also by the editors of *Cook's Illustrated*
Home of America's Test Kitchen

The Best Recipe
The Best Recipe: Grilling & Barbecue
The Best Recipe: Soups & Stews
American Classics
Italian Classics

Here in America's Test Kitchen
The America's Test Kitchen Cookbook

The Complete Book of Pasta and Noodles
The Cook's Illustrated Complete Book of Poultry

How to Barbecue and Roast on the Grill
How to Cook Chicken Breasts
How to Cook Chinese Favorites
How to Cook Garden Vegetables
How to Cook Shrimp and Other Shellfish
How to Grill
How to Make an American Layer Cake
How to Make Cookie Jar Favorites
How to Make Ice Cream
How to Make Muffins, Biscuits, and Scones
How to Make Pasta Sauces
How to Make Pot Pies and Casseroles
How to Make Salad
How to Make Sauces & Gravies
How to Make Simple Fruit Desserts
How to Make Soup
How to Make Stew
How to Sauté

http://www.cooksillustrated.com
http://www.americastestkitchen.com

The Best Kitchen Quick Tips

534 tricks, techniques, and shortcuts for the curious cook

By the editors of

COOK'S ILLUSTRATED

Illustrations by John Burgoyne

BOSTON COMMON PRESS

Brookline, Massachusetts

Boston Common Press
17 Station Street
Brookline, Massachusetts 02445

ISBN 0-936184-65-5
Library of Congress Cataloging-in-Publication Data
The editors of *Cook's Illustrated*
The Best Kitchen Quick Tips:
534 tricks, techniques, and shortcuts for the curious cook
1st Edition

ISBN 0-936184-65-5 $19.95
I. Cooking. I. Title
2003

Manufactured in the United States of America

Distributed by Boston Common Press, 17 Station Street, Brookline, MA 02445

Designed by Robin Gilmore-Barnes
Edited by Lori Galvin-Frost
Illustrated by John Burgoyne

ACKNOWLEDGMENTS

This book contains the most useful quick tips that have appeared in the pages of *Cook's Illustrated* since the charter issue was published in 1993. Many of the ideas illustrated in this book began as suggestions from readers. We are continually surprised by the ingenuity and common sense expressed in your letters, faxes, and e-mails.

For the past seven years, Adam Ried has been the person at the magazine who reads all of this correspondence and figures out which tips are unique enough to publish. He also writes the descriptive captions that bring the drawings to life.

Jack Bishop edits the magazine and his intelligence comes through in every quick tip.

The test kitchen staff tests the tips and adds its own refinements. Thanks to the efforts of Erika Bruce, Matthew Card, Julia Collin, Keith Dresser, Rebecca Hays, Bridget Lancaster, Erin McMurrer, Meg Suzuki, Nina West, and Dawn Yanagihara, you can be assured that these tips really work.

Lori Galvin-Frost combed through the thousands of drawings published in the magazine and turned the best tips into a coherent book. Talented designer Robin Gilmore-Barnes designed a book that is as attractive as it is easy to use. This project would not exist without the drawings of illustrator John Burgoyne. Over the years, his graceful, clear, and informative illustrations have told stories no words ever could.

The art, editorial, and production staffs worked long hours to produce this book. Special thanks to Ron Bilodeau, Barbara Bourassa, Rich Cassidy, Sharyn Chabot, Mary Connelly, Cathy Dorsey, Lenira DosReis, Freddy Flores, Larisa Greiner, Rebecca Hays, Amy Klee, India Koopman, Jim McCormack, Jennifer McCreary, Amy Monaghan, Nicole Morris, Henrietta Murray, Jessica Quirk, Jean Rogers, and Mandy Shito. And without help from members of the marketing staff, readers might never find our books. Special thanks to Deborah Broide, Steven Browall, Shekinah Cohn, Connie Forbes, Julie Gardner, Jason Geller, David Mack, Adam Perry, Steven Sussman, Jacqui Valerio, and Jonathan Venier. All contributed to our marketing and distribution efforts.

CONTENTS

INTRODUCTION

What is a quick tip? For the editors of *Cook's Illustrated,* it's an easier way of performing a kitchen task that either saves time or money or improves the quality of the outcome. The tip may call for an odd appliance such as a hair dryer (for smoothing chocolate frosting), a surprising ingredient such as miniature marshmallows (placed on the ends of toothpicks to hold plastic wrap above a frosted cake), or a common kitchen tool such as an egg slicer, which can be used to slice mushrooms.

These tips are the best picks from thousands of techniques and shortcuts submitted by our readers over the past eight years. You will find practical tricks for peeling tomatoes, mincing garlic, and organizing your pantry along with truly original ideas for getting the lumps out of polenta (use an immersion blender), knowing when your steamer is out of water (add marbles to the bottom of the pot), and toasting pine nuts without burning them (use a popcorn popper).

You will also find two of my favorite tips: use a coffee maker to melt chocolate and store natural peanut butter upside down so the oil doesn't separate and float to the top.

If you like this book, please join us at *Cook's Illustrated* by contacting us at www.cooksillustrated.com. Submit one of your quick tips, subscribe to the magazine, or ask a question on our bulletin board.

All the best,

Christopher Kimball
Editor and Publisher
Cook's Illustrated

Almond Paste – Butter

Almond paste is expensive and seldom used, which means that leftovers often sit around and harden before they can be used. When faced with hard-as-a-rock almond paste, try this softening method.

Almond Paste
SOFTENING

Place a slice of fresh bread in a bag with the almond paste and seal. The moisture from the bread will restore the almond paste to its original pliable state.

Anchovies
MINCING

Anchovies often stick to the side of a chef's knife,
making it hard to cut them into small bits. Here are two better
ways to mince anchovies.

Tip 2

Use a dinner fork to mash
delicate anchovy fillets into a
paste. Mash the fillets on a
small plate to catch any oil
the anchovies give off.

Tip 3

A garlic press will turn
anchovies into a fine puree.
This method is especially
handy when you have already
dirtied the press with garlic.

Many apples lose
their shape when
baked. Among common
varieties, we find that
Golden Delicious
apples bake up best.
Other good choices
include Baldwin,
Cortland, Ida Red,
and Northern Spy.

Apples
BAKING

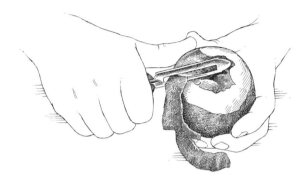

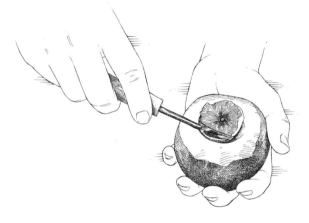

❶ To allow steam to escape
and to keep the apples from
bursting in the oven, remove
a strip of skin around each
apple's stem with a vegetable
peeler. Leave the rest of the
skin on the apple. We find
that the skin helps the apple
retain its shape in the oven.

❷ Removing the inedible
core gives you a chance to
stuff a baked apple with
brown sugar, nuts, or raisins.
The easiest way to core a
whole apple is with a melon
baller. Just be careful not to
puncture the blossom end or
the filling may leak out from
the bottom of the apple.

| **Apples and Pears**
EASY CORING

Many cooks like to use fresh-picked pears or apples in crisps, cakes, and the like. Coring the fruit can be accomplished quickly and easily with kitchen tools commonly found in the utensil drawer.

Tip 5

A melon baller is just the right size and shape to carve out the core cleanly and easily.

Tip 6

Alternatively, a sturdy rounded metal ½ teaspoon measure will core just as well.

Artichokes
STEAMING

Whole, trimmed artichokes should remain upright when steamed so that the leaves on one side don't cook faster than the leaves on the other side. So it is imperative the stuffed artichokes don't tip over. Here's an easy way to steady artichokes as they steam.

Cut very thick slices (about 1½ inches) from medium onions and use your fingers to remove the outer three or four rings from the rest of the slice. Set the onion rings on the bottom of the pan, and place one artichoke on each ring. In addition to steadying the artichoke, the onion lifts the stem end off the bottom of the pot and keeps it from overcooking. You can use the band from a canning jar lid in the same fashion.

Asparagus
TRIMMING THE TOUGH ENDS

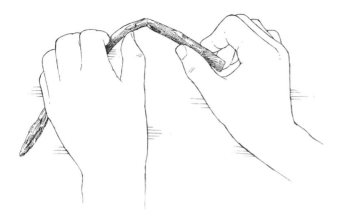

Tip 8

The tough, woody part of the stem will break off in just the right place—without cutting—if you hold the spear the right way.

With one hand, hold the asparagus about halfway down the stalk; with the thumb and index finger of the other hand, hold the spear about an inch up from the bottom. Bend the stalk until it snaps.

Tip 9

Avocados
TESTING FOR RIPENESS

We find that Hass avocados (the variety with dark, pebbly skin) are creamier and more flavorful than large, smooth-skinned varieties. Squeeze the avocado to judge ripeness. The flesh should yield to moderate pressure.

A soft avocado is sometimes bruised rather than truly ripe. To be sure, flick the small stem of the avocado. If it comes off easily and you can see green underneath it, the avocado is ripe. If the stem does not come off or if you see brown underneath it, the avocado is not ripe.

Avocados
PITTING

Tip 10

Digging out the pit with a spoon can mar the flesh and is generally a messy proposition. This method solves the problem.

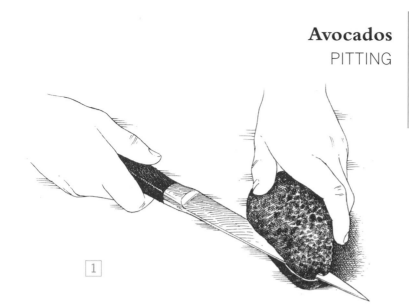

1

❶ Start by slicing around the pit and through both ends with a chef's knife.

❷ With your hands, twist the avocado to separate the two halves. Stick the blade of the chef's knife sharply into the pit. Lift the knife, twisting the blade if necessary to loosen and remove the pit.

❸ Don't pull the pit off the knife with your hands. Instead, use a large wooden spoon to pry the pit safely off the knife.

2

3

Once an avocado has been pitted, you may want to remove neat slices, especially for salads.

Avocados
SLICING

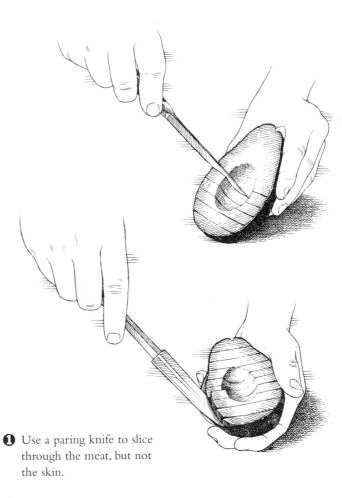

❶ Use a paring knife to slice through the meat, but not the skin.

❷ Run a rubber spatula around the circumference, just inside the skin, to loosen the avocado flesh. Once the flesh has been loosened from the skin, twist the spatula to pop out the meat.

Bacon

STORING

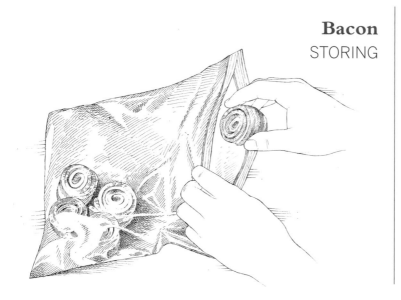

Now that many people eat bacon less often and in smaller amounts, it can be difficult to use up a pound, once opened, before it becomes rancid. Freezing is the best way to preserve bacon, but if frozen in the original package, it's impossible to later remove just a few slices at a time.

To solve this dilemma, roll up the bacon in tight cylinders, each with two to four slices of bacon. Place the cylinders in a zipper-lock plastic bag and place the bag flat in the freezer. (Once the slices are frozen, the bag can be stored as you like.) When bacon is needed, simply pull out the desired number of slices and defrost.

Tip 13

Bacon Drippings

SAVING FOR ANOTHER USE

Bacon grease lends a prized flavor to many dishes, especially Southern ones. Instead of keeping a bulky jar in the refrigerator, we like to store bacon drippings in the freezer.

Melt the collected drippings in the microwave and **❶** ▶ let the solids settle at the bottom of the bowl. Pour the fat through a fine-mesh sieve, keeping the solids in the bowl. (The solids can burn when the fat is reheated and are best discarded.)

Tip 14

Bacon Grease
REMOVAL

Even after pouring off bacon grease, there may still be some stubborn fat clinging to the pan. Here's a way to remove more of the fat, so it doesn't end up making your sink and wash cloth greasy.

After pouring off the bacon grease, crumple up a wad of paper towels, grab it with tongs, and use it to swab the extra grease from the pan. You might need a couple of wads depending on how much grease is in the pan.

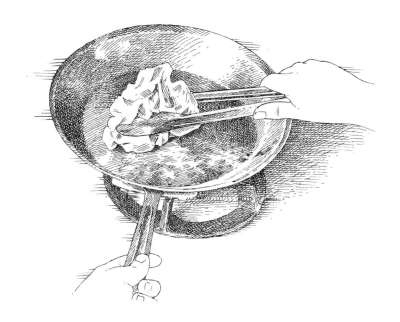

❷ Pour the strained fat into an ice cube tray and freeze. When frozen, pop out the cubes and transfer them to a zipper-lock plastic bag to prevent freezer burn. Each cube will be approximately one heaping tablespoon.

Tip 15

It can be difficult to shape stiff dough, especially for bagels, into rings. Rather than trying to roll the dough into ropes and attach the ends (which may not stick together), try this method.

Bagels
SHAPING A STIFF DOUGH INTO RINGS

1

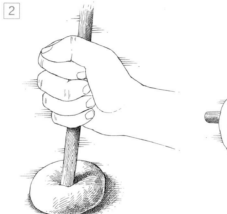

2

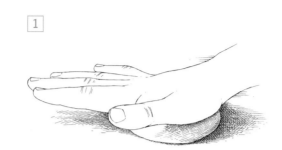

3

4

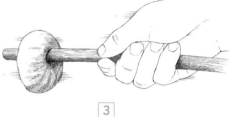

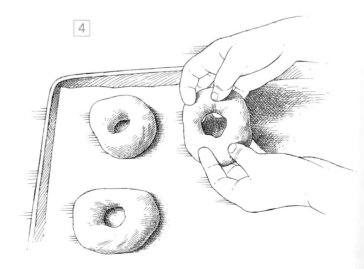

❶ Slightly flatten each ball of dough with the palm of your hand.

❷ Punch through the center of the ball with the handle of a wooden spoon.

❸ Holding the spoon by the handle, spin it gently to enlarge the dough ring to the desired size.

❹ Stretch the hole with your fingers as you place the dough ring on a baking sheet.

Baking
KEEPING TRACK OF DRY INGREDIENTS

When a recipe calls for a number of dry ingredients to be added simultaneously (such as baking powder, baking soda, salt, and spices), it's easy to lose track of what's been added to the bowl, especially if you get interrupted.

Place the measured ingredients in separate mounds on a sheet of parchment or waxed paper. This way you can see not only what but also how much you have measured.

Baking
MEASURING LIQUIDS

Holding a cup may jostle or tilt the liquid and can destroy the accuracy of the measurements that might make all the difference when baking.

To avoid possible mis-measurements, pour liquids into clear measuring cups set on the counter and lean down to read them at eye level.

Accomplished and novice bakers alike know that the traditional method of greasing and flouring cake pans can be a bit of a nuisance. Save yourself some work by using this all-in-one baker's coating.

Mix 2 parts shortening with 1 part flour and brush this paste lightly onto the cake pans. Store the mixture at room temperature in a plastic resealable container, so you'll have the coating on hand when the need arises.

Baking
MESS-FREE BAKER'S COATING

Baking
SLIP-FREE PARCHMENT PAPER

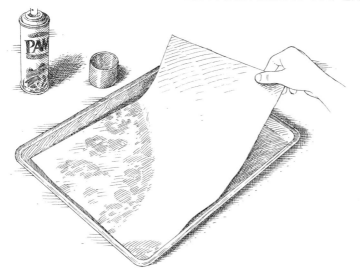

Parchment can often slip and slide over a baking sheet, so it's helpful to anchor it to the pan.

Spray the baking pan with a light coating of cooking spray. The parchment paper will adhere to the sticky surface, and cleanup will be quick and easy.

Baking Powder
TESTING FOR FRESHNESS

Baking powder will lose its leavening ability with time. If the can is not marked with an expiration date, we suggest writing the date the can was opened on a piece of tape. Affix the tape to the bottom of the can. After six months, baking powder will begin to weaken, and after a year it should be discarded. If you have any doubts about the strength of your baking powder, use this test.

Mix 2 teaspoons of baking powder with 1 cup of hot tap water. If there's an immediate reaction of fizzing and foaming (right), the baking powder can be used. If the reaction is at all delayed or weak (left), throw the baking powder away and buy a fresh can.

Bananas

SAVING OVERRIPE FRUIT FOR BREAD

Tip 21

Rather than throwing away one or two overripe bananas, save them until you have enough fruit to make banana bread.

Place overripe bananas in a zipper-lock plastic bag and freeze them. As needed, add more bananas to the bag. When you are ready to make bread, thaw the bananas on the counter until softened.

Tip 22

Barbecue Sauce

APPLYING WITH A SQUEEZE BOTTLE

Instead of brushing barbecue sauce onto foods and dirtying both the brush and bowl, recycle a pull-top water bottle by filling it with sauce and keeping it in the refrigerator until needed.

When the chicken, pork chop, or other food is almost done, squirt a little sauce onto the food, taking care not to let the bottle touch the food. Wipe the bottle clean and store it in the refrigerator until needed again.

Basil
RELEASING FLAVORFUL OILS

It's easy to make pesto in a food processor or blender, but the fast grinding action of the blades doesn't create the richest tasting sauce. For the fullest flavor in pesto and other sauces, we find it best to bruise basil leaves before placing them in a food processor or blender. This trick also works with other soft herbs, especially mint and cilantro.

Place the basil leaves in a zipper-lock plastic bag and bruise with a meat pounder or rolling pin.

Bean Sprouts
KEEPING THEM CRISP AND FRESH

Bean sprouts are prized for their crunch. To keep them crisp, try this tip, which also works with peeled jícama slices.

Submerge the sprouts in a container of cold water, then refrigerate the container. The sprouts will stay crisp for up to five days.

Beef *Kebabs*
PREPARING THE MEAT

Cut the meat into large cubes. Cut each cube almost through at the center, making sure to leave the meat attached on one side. The meat is ready to be marinated.

Tip 25

Top blade and top sirloin are the best cuts for kebabs. Butterflying the cubes almost through at the center before marinating creates more surface area so the marinade can penetrate the meat in a shorter amount of time, thus resulting in faster, more flavorful kebabs. This method also produces a less chewy kebab that's easier to eat.

Tip 26

In the oven, the outer layer of meat often pulls away from the rib-eye muscle and overcooks.

To prevent this problem, tie the roast at both ends, running the kitchen twine parallel to the bone.

Beef *Prime Rib*
TYING UP A ROAST

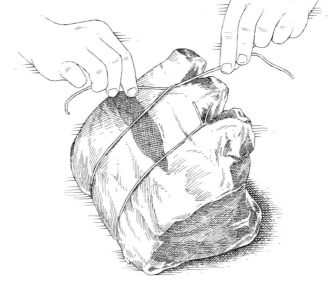

Most instant-read
thermometers work best
when the tip is stuck at
least an inch deep into
foods. On a thin steak, the
tip can go right through
the meat if inserted from
the top. Use this tip for
steaks as well as chops.

Beef *Steak*

CHECKING THE INTERNAL TEMPERATURE

For the most accurate reading, hold the steak with a pair of tongs and slide the tip of the thermometer through the side of the steak. Make sure that the shaft is embedded in the meat and not touching any bone. The steak is done when the temperature registers 120 degrees for rare, 125 to 130 degrees for medium-rare, or 135 to 140 degrees for medium.

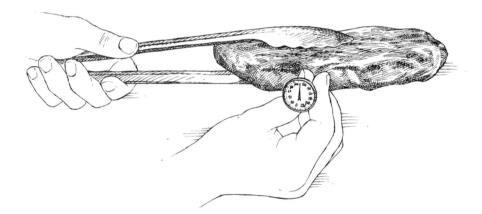

T-bone and porterhouse steaks contain portions of the delicate, buttery tenderloin as well as some of the chewier, more flavorful strip. With the two cuts of meat, these steaks are especially enjoyable to eat but somewhat challenging to cook. A two-level fire (see tip 257, page 186), with more coals banked to one side than the other, helps even out the rate at which these two muscles cook.

Beef *Steak*

GRILLING T-BONE STEAKS EVENLY

When grilling T-bone or porterhouse steaks, keep the tenderloin (the smaller portion to the left of the bone) over the cooler part of the fire. The strip (the larger portion to the right of the bone) should be placed over the hotter part of the fire.

A thick T-bone or porterhouse steak weighs between 1½ and 2 pounds, too much for a single serving. Here's how to serve one steak to two people. Once cooked, let the steak rest for five minutes so the juices can redistribute themselves evenly throughout the meat.

Beef *Steak*
SLICING T-BONE STEAKS

❶ Start by slicing close to the bone to remove the larger strip section.

❷ Turn the steak around and cut the smaller tenderloin section off the bone.

❸ Cut each piece crosswise into ⅓-inch-thick slices. Make sure each person gets some tenderloin as well as some strip meat.

It's not necessary to own a meat slicer to make a good Philly steak sandwich. You can cut paper-thin pieces of steak, ready to be thrown onto a hot, oiled griddle, by starting with partially frozen sirloin, blade, or round steaks and employing your food processor.

Beef *Steak*
PREPARING PHILLY STEAK SANDWICH MEAT

❶ Trim the fat from the steaks and cut into 1-inch-wide strips. Freeze the meat until the exterior hardens but the interior remains soft and yields to gentle pressure, 25 to 50 minutes.

❷ Once the meat has been partially frozen, place the strips in the feed tube of a food processor fitted with the slicing disk. Turn on the food processor, and use the plunger to push the meat down into the blade.

❸ The food processor will shave the meat into small, paper-thin pieces.

Flank steak is our favorite cut for stir-fries. It has the right balance of tenderness (with some chew) and beef flavor. It must be sliced as thinly as possible, so a sharp knife is essential. Freezing the meat for 30 to 60 minutes also helps.

Beef *Stir-Fries*
SLICING FLANK STEAK THINLY

Slice the partially frozen ❶ flank steak into 2-inch-wide pieces.

Cut each piece of flank ❷ steak against the grain into very thin slices.

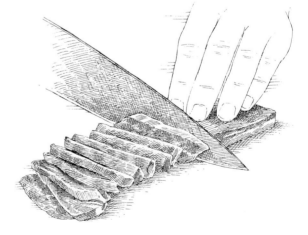

Beef *Tenderloin*
TYING TO ENSURE EVEN COOKING

Tip 32

The tenderloin narrows at one end, called the tip. If roasted or grilled as is, this end will be overcooked by the time the thicker end is done.

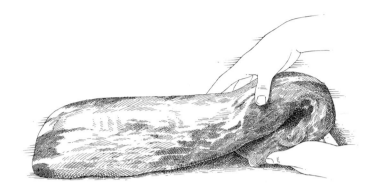

❶ To prevent overcooking, fold the last six inches of the thin tip end under the roast.

Tip 33

Beef *Tenderloin*
CUTTING THE SILVER SKIN

The tenderloin is covered with a thin, shiny membrane called the silver skin that can contract in the oven and cause the roast to bow. Rather than trying to peel off this very thin membrane, use this technique to keep it from bowing the meat. The same technique can be used with a pork tenderloin.

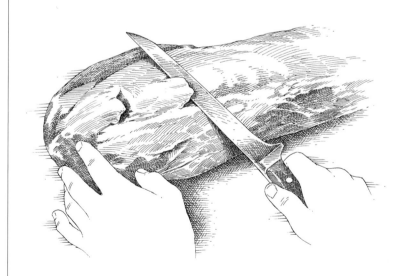

Slide a knife under the silver skin and flick the blade upward to cut through the membrane. Do this at five or six spots along the length of the roast.

❷ Tie 12-inch lengths of kitchen twine crosswise along the length of the roast, spacing the ties about 1½ inches apart.

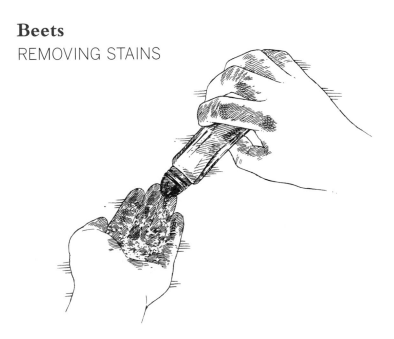

Tip 34

When cut, beets stain everything they touch, including hands and cutting boards.

Beets
REMOVING STAINS

To help remove these stains, sprinkle the stained area with salt, rinse, and then scrub with soap. The salt crystals help lift the beet juices away.

Tip 35

Berries
MIXING GENTLY

When making a fresh fruit salad or tart, it's nearly impossible to avoid crushing fresh berries in a mixing bowl, and it's even more difficult to keep them intact when you're trying to coat them with sugar. Try this method instead.

Place the berries in a large plastic bag and add the sugar, if using. Hold the bag closed with one hand, and use the other hand to gently jostle the berries to combine them. If using the berries in a tart, simply empty the bag directly into the pastry shell.

Beverages
KEEPING CHILLED

Tip 36

Refrigerator space for chilling beverages is often at a premium when you're throwing a party. Press another household appliance into action to solve the problem.

Use your washing machine as an icebox. Fill the washer's basket with ice cubes, then nestle in the cans and bottles. When it's time for more cold drinks, they're at the ready. When the party is over and the ice has melted, simply run the washer's spin cycle to drain the water.

Biscotti
QUICK-DRYING ON A RACK

Traditionally, biscotti dough is baked in a log, then cut into slices and baked a second time. These slices must be flipped halfway through the baking time to dry both sides of each slice. Here's how to streamline this method.

Bake the dough in a log as usual and then cut into slices. Place the slices on a wire cooling rack set on a cookie sheet and bake again. The rack elevates the slices, allowing air to circulate all around them and drying both sides at once.

There is no re-patting of biscuits when you use the wedge method—an economical and quick way to get biscuits ready for the oven. And there's no need for a biscuit cutter.

Biscuits
CUTTING WEDGE BISCUITS

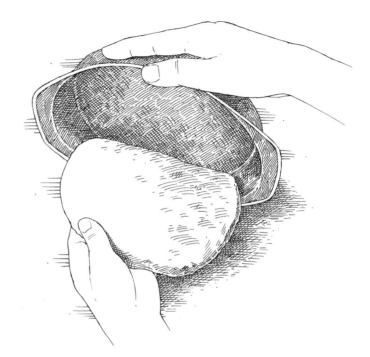

Press the dough into a round ❶ cake pan large enough so that the dough is ¾ inch thick. Turn the dough out onto a lightly floured work surface.

With a knife or bench ❷ scraper, cut the dough into equal-sized wedges.

Biscuits
SPLITTING FOR SHORTCAKES

It's important to split biscuits evenly when making shortcakes. A knife sometimes tears the biscuits and isn't necessarily the best tool for the job.

When the biscuits have cooled slightly, look for the crack that naturally forms around the circumference of each biscuit. Gently insert your fingers into the crack and split the biscuit in half.

Blanching
SHOCKING VEGETABLES IN A STRAINER

Vegetables, especially green ones, are often partially cooked in boiling water (a process called blanching) to set their color. The blanched vegetables are then "shocked" in ice water to stop the cooking process.

Drain the vegetables into a strainer, then plunge the strainer into a bowl of ice water. When the vegetables have cooled, lift the strainer from the ice water and let the water drain back into the bowl.

Blender
CLEANING THE JAR

Washing the blender jar can be a real chore, especially if foods have had time to harden. Get a head start on the cleaning process by following this method.

Fill the dirty blender ❶ halfway with hot water and add a couple of drops of liquid dish soap.

With the top firmly in place, ❷ turn the blender on high for 30 seconds. Most of the residue pours right out with the soapy water, and the blender jar need only be rinsed or lightly washed by hand.

Nooks, crannies, and crevices on the face of a blender pose a particular cleaning challenge. Here is an idea that makes the chore less cumbersome.

Use a nail brush to get in between the buttons or around the dials on your blender.

Blender
CLEANING THE FACE

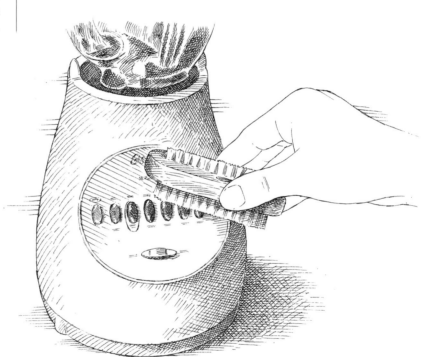

Bok Choy
SLICING WHITES AND GREENS

The thick, fleshy white stalks take much longer to cook than the tender, leafy greens. For this reason, you should slice them separately, so the whites can be added to a stir-fry or other dish first.

❶ Cut the leafy green portions of the bok choy away from either side of the white stalk.

❷ Cut each white stalk in half lengthwise and then crosswise.

❸ Stack the leafy greens and then slice them crosswise into thin strips. Keep the stalks and leaves separate.

1

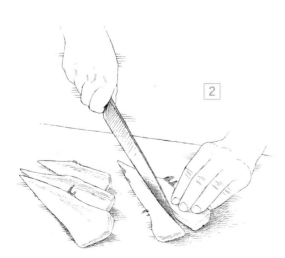

2

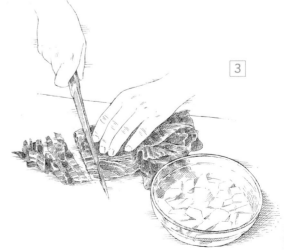

3

Bread
PERFECT SLICES FROM CRUSTY LOAVES

Artisan breads have heavy crusts that can be difficult to slice neatly. Often the bread knife fails to cut all the way through the thick bottom crust. The result is that you must yank the slice free from the loaf, often tearing it in the process. Here's how to slice a crusty loaf neatly.

Turn the loaf on its side and cut through the top and bottom crust simultaneously. The crust on the side of the bread, which is now facing down, is often thinner and easier to slice.

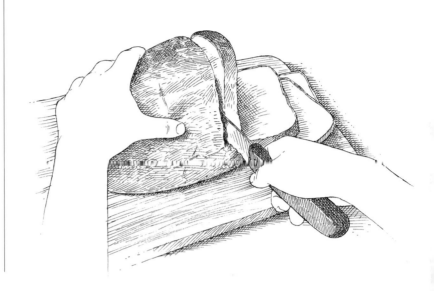

Bread
KEEPING BREAD FRESH

The twist ties that come with loaves of sandwich bread have an uncanny ability to disappear. Don't let your bread grow stale because of a lost tie.

Twist the bread bag shut and fold the excess back on itself, over the remaining bread. This works best after a few slices have been eaten.

We all know bread goes stale very quickly.
Here are two tricks for reviving slightly stale loaves and slices.
Neither trick will work with rock-hard, days-old bread.

Tip 46

Individual slices of stale bread can be freshened on a splatter screen held over a pan of simmering water. The rising steam will soften the bread in a minute or two.

Tip 47

Place a stale loaf of bread inside a brown paper bag, seal the bag, and lightly moisten the outside of the bag with some water. Place the bag on a baking sheet in a 350-degree oven for five minutes. When you remove the loaf, you will find it is warm and soft.

Bread
IMPROVISED LOAF PANS

Tip 48

If you own just one loaf pan but need to make two loaves at the same time, try this trick for improvising a second, or even third, pan.

Place a single loaf pan across **1** the center of a 9 by 13-inch baking dish.

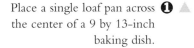

Position one portion of **2** shaped dough on either side of the loaf pan and bake. (Fill the loaf pan with a third portion of dough to bake three loaves.)

Bread *Making the Dough*
JUDGING WHEN BREAD HAS ENOUGH FLOUR

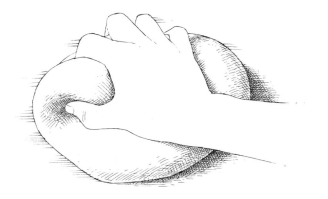

Many bakers add too much flour to bread dough, which results in dry loaves. Here's an easy test to see if your bread has enough flour.

Squeeze the dough gently with your entire hand. Even with especially soft, sticky doughs, your hand will pull away cleanly once the dough has enough flour.

Once the dough is ready to rise, most recipes suggest putting it into a deep bowl and covering the bowl with a damp kitchen towel. We find that the towel doesn't protect the dough from drafts.

Instead, tightly seal the bowl with plastic wrap, which keeps out drafts and traps moisture so the dough remains supple.

Bread *Rising and Shaping*
COVERING THE DOUGH

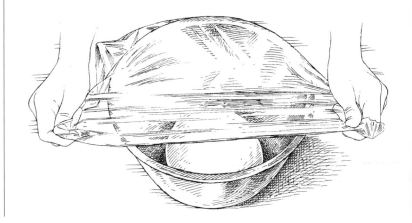

Bread *Rising and Shaping*
DRAFT-FREE RISING IN A LOAF PAN

Some doughs should rise right in a loaf pan just before baking. (This is called the second rise.) If your kitchen is drafty, the dough may not rise properly. Here's a defense against a drafty environment.

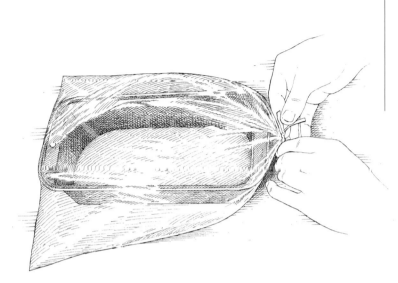

1 After forming the dough and placing it in a loaf pan, slip the pan into an empty plastic bag. Blow air into the bag to inflate it, then seal it securely with a twist tie.

2 Place this loaf pan into another loaf pan so that the air inside the bag is pushed up, providing room for the dough to expand.

Recipes often call for bread dough to be shaped to a specific length or pastry to be rolled to a specific size. Rather than fumbling in drawers with messy hands to find a ruler each time, put this tip to work.

Bread *Rising and Shaping*
MEASURING BREAD AND PASTRY DOUGHS

Affix a yardstick to the front of a countertop. It's not obtrusive, and it's always there when you need it. To measure doughs, simply line up the ends with markings on the ruler and do the math.

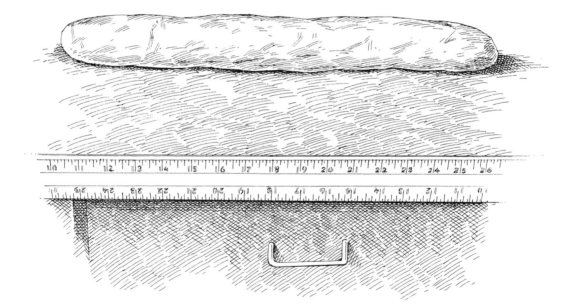

Bread
TRACKING DOUGH RISE

Tip 53

❶ After adding the dough to the container, mark its height by placing a rubber band around the container.

❷ This reference will make it easy to judge when the dough has doubled in volume.

Not every baker owns a dough-rising bucket with markings for tracking the rise of the dough, but any baker with a large, clear container can improvise one with this trick.

Bread

SLASHING A PROOFED LOAF NEATLY

Tip 54

A proofed loaf of bread should be slashed across the top to allow some of the trapped air to escape, but the knife used for this purpose often snags and drags the loaf out of shape.

For clean, neat slashes, spray the knife blade lightly with cooking spray before slashing the loaf.

Tip 55

Internal temperature is a good way to gauge whether or not a loaf of bread is done. Don't be tempted to pierce the top crust in the center, which will leave behind a conspicuous hole.

Insert the thermometer from the side, just above the edge of the loaf pan, directing it at a downward angle toward the center of the loaf.

Bread *Baking*

TAKING THE TEMPERATURE IN A LOAF PAN

Bread
QUICK RELEASE FOR QUICK BREADS

Tip 56

Although we use nonstick cooking spray on our loaf pans when making quick breads, we also like to add a layer of parchment for extra assurance.

❶ Make a sling for the loaf by laying long wide strips of parchment paper across the length and width of the pan so that the paper overlaps the edges.

❷ Use the overlap as a handy grip when it's time to remove the loaf from the pan.

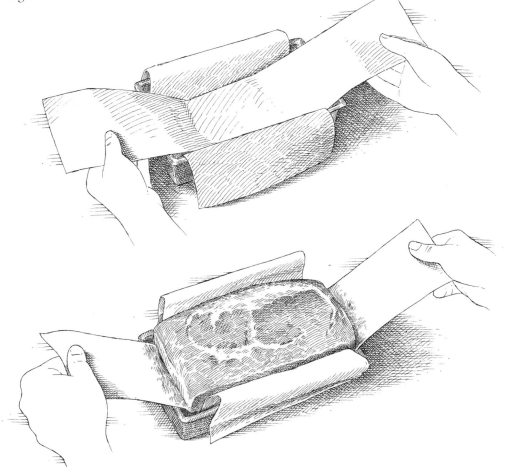

Bread Crumbs
SLICING OFF THE TOUGH BOTTOM CRUST

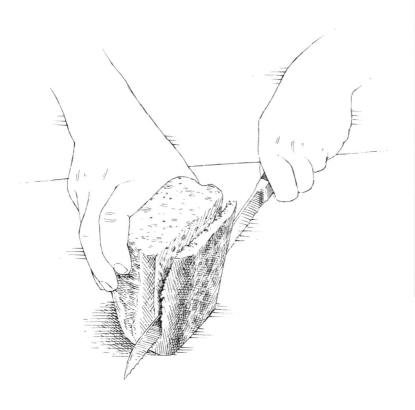

Homemade bread crumbs are far superior to commercial dry crumbs. To make your own crumbs, simply grind cubes of stale bread in a food processor until coarsely chopped. There's one hitch: Many loaves of bread have a thick bottom crust that won't break down in a food processor.

To prevent this problem, simply slice off and discard the bottom crust before cutting the bread into large cubes that will fit in the food processor.

| # Broccoli
TWO WAYS TO REMOVE FLORETS

Some heads of broccoli have closely bunched branches
that meet the central stalk at roughly the same point. On other heads, the branches
are widely spaced. You should adjust the way you remove florets depending
on how a head of broccoli is shaped.

Tip 58

Lay a head of broccoli
with closely bunched
branches on its side, and
use a chef's knife to cut off
the florets about ½ inch
below their heads.

Tip 59

❶ When working with a
head of broccoli with widely
spaced branches, stand the
broccoli upside down and use
a chef's knife to trim off the
florets close to their heads.

❷ Break the large florets into
bite-sized pieces, snapping
them apart where individual
clusters meet.

When we tried to skim the blob of fat from canned broth with a spoon, it always broke into little pieces, making it difficult to remove it all. We found the answer to foolproof skimming with this simple, quick method.

Broth
DEFATTING CANNED BROTH

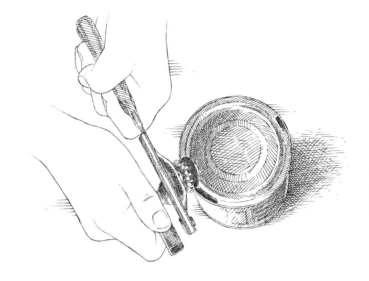

Using a manual can opener, ❶ ▷ punch a small hole in the top of the can without turning. Rotate the can 180 degrees and make a second opening about ½ to 1 inch long.

Pour the stock through the ❷ ▷ larger opening. The liquid will pass through, but the more viscous fat will remain trapped in the can.

Brown Sugar
SOFTENING

Place a cup or so of brown sugar in a glass pie plate or bowl, cover with a small piece of waxed paper, and then top with a slice of bread to provide a bit of moisture. Loosely cover the pie plate or bowl with plastic wrap and microwave until softened, about 30 seconds.

Tip 61

There's nothing worse than hardened brown sugar, which is impossible to measure and can't be incorporated into batters. Here's how to bring back its original texture.

Pouring brown sugar out of its narrow box into a measuring cup can be a messy, frustrating chore. This method will not only make measuring easier, but will help the sugar remain moist.

Brown Sugar
STORING AND MEASURING

Transfer the brown sugar from the box to a large, heavy-duty zipper-lock bag. A measuring cup will fit inside the bag easily and can be loaded up by pressing the sugar into it through the plastic. No pouring, spilling, or sticky hands.

Brownies
EASY REMOVAL FROM PANS

Tip 63

It can be difficult to extract fudgy brownies and bar cookies from baking pans. Parchment helps solves this problem and makes cleanup a breeze.

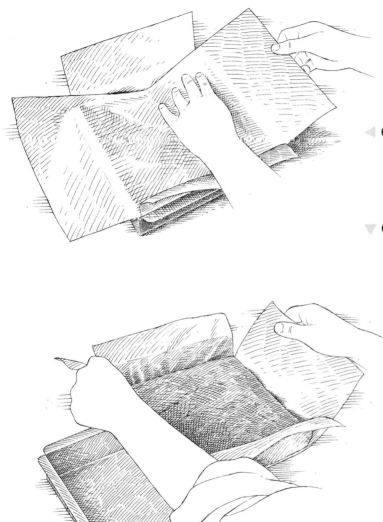

❶ Place two parchment sheets perpendicular to each other in the pan. Scrape the batter into the pan, pushing it into the corners.

❷ After the brownies or bars have baked and cooled, use the parchment to transfer them to a cutting board, then slice into individual portions.

Brushes
GETTING THEM CLEAN

It can be very difficult to clean a basting brush that has been dipped in oil or sauce. As a result, the bristles often remain sticky and sometimes even get smelly as the brush sits in a drawer between uses. Here's a better way to care for your brushes.

Wash the dirty brushes thoroughly with liquid dish soap and very hot water, then rinse well and shake dry. Place the brushes, bristles pointing down, into a cup and fill the cup with coarse salt until the bristles are covered. The salt draws moisture out of the bristles and keeps them dry and fresh between uses. The next time you need a brush, simply shake off the salt, and you're ready to go.

Burgers
GETTING AN ACCURATE TEMPERATURE READING

It's hard to get an accurate temperature reading even in the thickest burgers. While we like to hold steaks and chops with tongs and slide an instant-read thermometer through the side (see tip 27, page 19), we find this technique can cause delicate burgers to break apart.

Instead, slide the tip of the thermometer into the burger at the top edge and push it toward the center.

Butter

TABLESPOONS AT THE READY

Tip 66

Measured tablespoons of softened butter are at the ready with this method.

When unwrapping a new stick of butter, cut it into tablespoons (using the markings on the wrapper as a guide) before placing it in the butter dish. The smaller pieces will soften faster than an entire stick and there's no last-minute measuring.

Butter
MAKING COMPOUND BUTTERS

Use of compound butters (softened butters mixed with chopped herbs, citrus zest, minced ginger or garlic, and other seasonings) is a quick way to add rich flavor to grilled or roasted fish, chicken, chops, or steaks. Once the butter has been shaped, it can be wrapped and frozen for up to three months.

❶ Place the compound butter on top of a piece of waxed paper.

❷ Roll the butter into a long, narrow cylinder. Transfer the paper-wrapped cylinder to a zipper-lock plastic bag and freeze.

When you need it, take the ❸ butter out of the freezer, unwrap it, and cut off rounds about ½ inch thick. Place the rounds on top of freshly cooked hot foods and let them melt as you carry plates to the table.

Tip 68

Many recipes for casseroles and pies direct the cook to dot the surface with butter just before putting the dish into the oven. Instead of dicing butter (which is a messy proposition), try this neater method.

Butter

SHAVING THIN SLICES OVER CASSEROLES

Use a vegetable peeler to shave the desired amount from a frozen stick of butter, letting the pieces fall onto the food in fine curls.

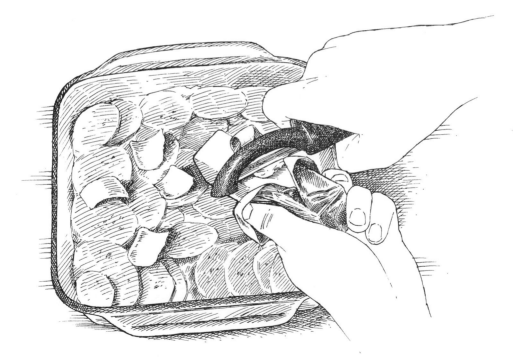

Butter

GRATING BUTTER INTO FLOUR

Many cooks use their fingertips to cut butter into flour, but the heat from one's hands can cause the butter to melt. We think the food processor is the best tool for cutting butter into flour to make pie pastry or biscuits, but if you don't have a food processor, try this method.

Rub a frozen stick of butter ❶ 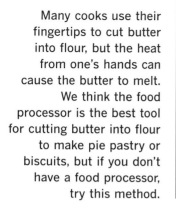 against the large holes of a regular box grater over the bowl with the flour.

Once all the butter has been ❷ grated, use a pastry blender or two table knives to work the butter into the flour. Keep cutting in the butter until the pieces are pea-sized.

Butter

GAUGING PROPERLY SOFTENED BUTTER

Tip 70

To cream butter for cookies or cakes, the butter must be brought to cool room temperature (about 67 degrees) so that it is malleable but not soft. Don't hurry this step. Cold butter can't hold as much air as properly softened butter, and the resulting cakes and cookies may be too dense. If you don't have an instant-read thermometer to take the temperature of butter, use these visual clues.

When you unwrap **❶** ▲ the butter, the wrapping should have a creamy residue on the inside. If there's no residue, the butter is probably too cold.

The butter should bend with **❷** ▶ little resistance and without cracking or breaking.

The butter should give **❸** ▶ slightly when pressed but still hold its shape.

Butter

SOFTENING BUTTER IN A HURRY

It can take a long time for a stick of chilled butter to reach the right temperature for creaming. Many cooks are tempted to use the microwave, but this is an imperfect solution because the edges of the butter often begin to melt before the center is really softened. If you are in a hurry, cut the butter into tablespoon-sized pieces. It will be soft enough to use in about 15 minutes.

If, despite all precautions, your butter is still too cool, a quick remedy is to wrap the bowl with a warm, damp towel and continue creaming.

Cabbage — Cutting Board

Cabbage
CUTTING THROUGH A BIG HEAD

Because most heads of cabbage are at least the size of your chef's knife, it can be hard to figure out how to cut them.

Start by placing the heel of ❶ ▷ your palm on the back of the knife, a little in front of center, and applying pressure toward the tip of the knife as it goes into the cabbage.

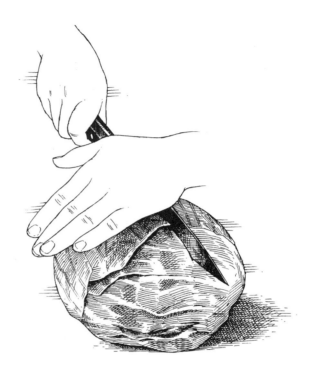

◁ ❷ Once the blade is completely below the top of the cabbage, move your fingers to the top of the front section of the knife and apply pressure to finish cutting.

Cabbage
TWO WAYS TO SHRED

For many recipes, including coleslaw, cabbage should be cut into long, thin strips. This process is called shredding. Start by cutting the cabbage into quarters (see tip 72, page 56).

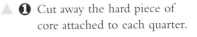

❶ Cut away the hard piece of core attached to each quarter.

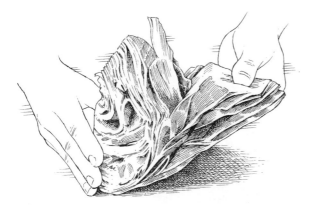

❷ Separate the cored cabbage quarters into stacks of leaves that flatten when pressed lightly.

(continued on page 58)

(Cabbage | Two Ways to Shred, continued from page 57)

❸ From here you have two choices:

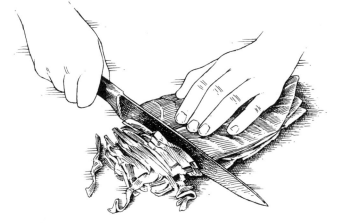

Tip 73

Use a chef's knife to cut each stack diagonally (this ensures long pieces) into thin shreds.

Tip 74

Or, roll the stacked leaves crosswise to fit them into the feed tube of a food processor fitted with a shredding disk.

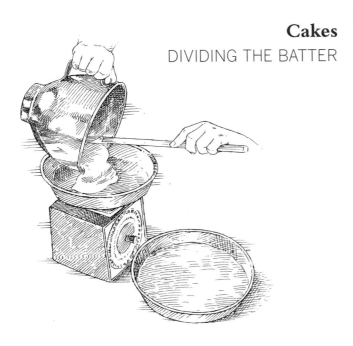

Cakes
DIVIDING THE BATTER

It's important to divide cake batter evenly between pans so that the layers are the same height when baked. Eyeballing the amount of batter can be tricky.

To ensure that you put equal amounts of batter in each cake pan, use a kitchen scale to measure the weight of each filled pan.

Cakes
FILLING TUBE PANS WITH BATTER

Many bakers know the frustration of spilling batter down the hole in the center of a tube pan. Here's how to keep the batter from running inside the tube, where it can burn and cause a mess.

After the pan has been prepared (greased and/or lined with parchment paper), set a small paper cup over the center tube. You can then scrape the batter into the pan without worrying that some may end up in the tube.

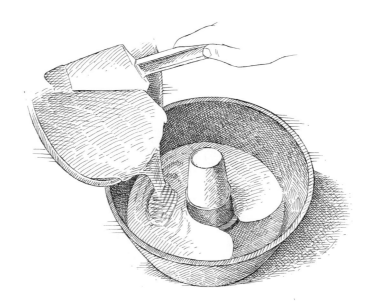

Cakes
LINING THE PAN AND SERVING PLATTER

Most recipes call for lining cake pans with parchment paper to ensure easy removal. It's also a good idea to line a serving plate with parchment paper before decorating the cake so that excess frosting and nuts do not dirty the plate. The paper is removed once you've finished decorating. Here's how to use one piece of parchment to do both jobs.

Tip 78

Cakes
ROTATING DURING BAKING

Most bakers know that cakes need to be rotated during baking to ensure even browning, but a hand clad in a bulky oven mitt can easily mar the surface of a cake. Here's a better method to rotate your cake.

Use a pair of kitchen tongs, which easily grasp the lip of the cake pan without touching the surface of the cake.

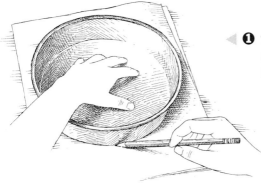

❶ Trace the bottom of your cake pan roughly in the center of a sheet of parchment paper.
(Use a double sheet if making two cake layers.)

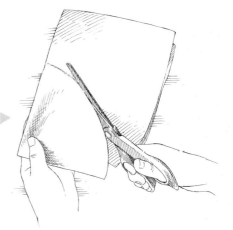

❷ Fold the traced circle in half and then in half again, then cut just inside the outline of the quarter circle. The resulting round of parchment will fit your pan exactly.

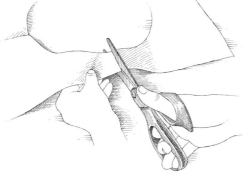

❸ Cut the remainder of the sheet in half so that it makes an adjustable circle.

❹ This circle will fit perfectly around the cake on the serving plate, keeping the plate rim neat while you frost and decorate.

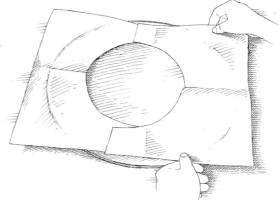

Cakes

TESTING FOR DONENESS

When testing an especially deep or thick cake, such as a Bundt cake, chiffon cake, or angel food cake, a toothpick won't be long enough and a knife will create too big a hole. Here's how to test whether crumbs cling without marring the surface too much.

Stick an uncooked strand of spaghetti or a thin skewer deep into the center of the cake and remove. If the tester is covered with moist batter, the cake needs more time in the oven.

Tip 80

When you want to make a cake with more than two layers, you will need to split the baked layers in half horizontally. However, if you cut the layers a bit unevenly (which is bound to happen), the cake can lean to one side or the other. Here's a neat trick that helps compensate for less-than-perfect cutting.

Cakes
ALIGNING THE LAYERS

Place the cooled cake layers ❶ ▷ on top of each other and make a ⅛-inch-deep cut down the side of each cake layer with a serrated knife.

Split the cake layers, and then ❷ ▷ begin to fill and assemble the cake, realigning the vertical cuts in the side of each layer. By putting the layers back in their original orientation to each other, you will conceal any unevenness in the way you cut them.

Cakes *Frosting*
ANCHORING THE BOTTOM LAYER

Once the cake layers have cooled, it's time to frost them. We find it best to frost a cake on a cardboard round cut slightly larger than the cake layers. The cardboard supports the cake and makes it easy to move around.

Use a dab of frosting to anchor the cake layer to the cardboard round.

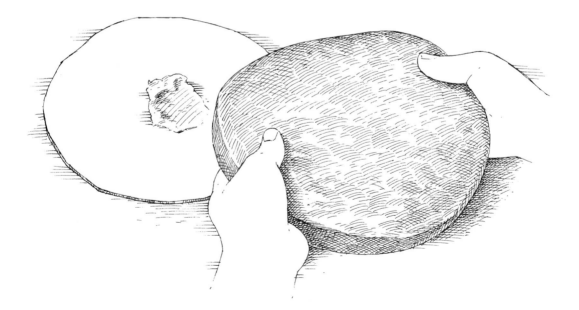

It can be tricky to lift a
top cake layer into place.
If you use your hands,
the layer may break.
Here's a safe way to
position the top layer.

Cakes *Frosting*
PLACING THE TOP LAYER

Place the layer on a cardboard
round or on the removable
bottom of a tart pan, then
slide the layer into place.

Cakes *Frosting*
PUTTING A PATTERN IN THE ICING

Once a cake has been frosted, there are several ways to style the icing.

Tip 83

Use the tines of a dinner fork to make wave designs in the icing. Wipe the fork clean intermittently. You can make this pattern on the top of the cake or on the top and sides.

Tip 84

Use the back of a large dinner spoon to make swirls on top of the cake.

Tip 85

Use the tip of a thin, metal icing spatula to stipple the top and sides of the cake.

Cakes *Frosting*
CREATING A SILKY LOOK

Professionally decorated cakes seem to have a molten, silky look.

To get that same appearance at home, frost as usual and then use a hair dryer to "blow-dry" the frosted surface of the cake. The slight melting of the frosting gives it that smooth, lustrous appearance.

Powdered sugar and cocoa powder can be used singly or in combination to give a frosted cake a polished look. When using stencils of any sort, freeze the cake for 15 minutes before decorating. Powdered sugar will gradually dissolve, so apply this fancy decoration just before serving.

Cakes *Decorating*
USING JAR LIDS TO MAKE A TWO-TONE PATTERN

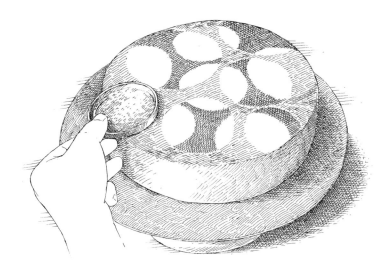

❶ Gather six jar lids, varying in size from small to medium. Place the lids face down on the surface of the cake in a random arrangement, letting some hang over the edge. Dust the cake with cocoa or confectioners' sugar.

❷ Remove the lids, grasping them by the lip and lifting straight up. Rearrange them randomly again, then dust with a contrasting color, using confectioners' sugar, cocoa, or very finely ground nuts. Remove the lids carefully.

The shape and color of sliced almonds lend them to simple, elegant designs.
Here are two tips that can be used singly or in combination.

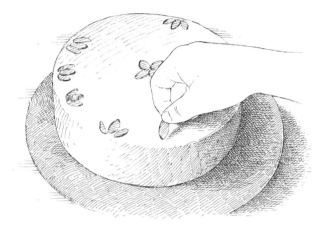

Tip 88

Arrange sliced almonds in a fleur-de-lis design around the perimeter of the cake. Use four slices to make a flower design in the center of the cake.

Tip 89

To press nuts onto the sides of the cake, lift the cake off the stand or counter and hold it by the cardboard round underneath. Use one hand to hold the cake above a bowl containing nuts; use the other hand to press the nuts into the icing, letting the excess fall back into the bowl. You will need about 1 cup of nuts to cover the sides of a 9-inch layer cake. You can use sliced almonds (as pictured) or chopped pecans or walnuts.

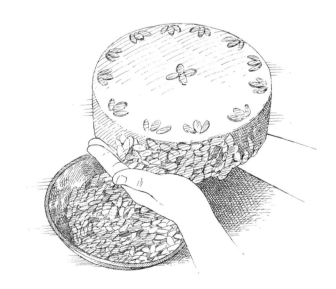

Cakes *Decorating*
APPLYING CHOCOLATE SHAVINGS

Tip 90

If the chocolate is too hard, it can be difficult to pull off thick shavings. Even if you do cut off nice shavings, warmth from your fingers can cause the pieces to melt as you try to place them on the cake. Here's how to avoid both problems.

Warm a block of bittersweet ❶ ▲ or semisweet chocolate by sweeping a hair dryer over it, taking care not to melt the chocolate. Holding a paring knife at a 45-degree angle against the chocolate, scrape toward you, anchoring the block with your other hand.

Pick up the shavings with a ❷ ▶ toothpick and place them as desired on the frosted cake.

When writing a
message on top of a
frosted cake, it's easiest
to use chocolate on a
light-colored frosting.

Cakes *Decorating*
WRITING ON FROSTING

1 Put semisweet or bittersweet
chocolate in a zipper-lock
plastic bag and immerse the
bag in hot water until the
chocolate melts. Dry the bag,
then snip off a small piece
from one corner.

2 Holding the bag in one hand,
gently squeeze the chocolate
out of the hole as you write.

Cakes *Decorating*
REMOVING STENCILS

Tip 92

Using a store-bought stencil (available in most kitchen shops) is an easy way to decorate an unfrosted cake. The problem is removing the stencil without marring the design.

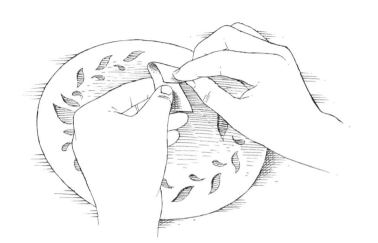

❶ Create two handles for the stencil by folding two short lengths of masking tape back on themselves, pinching the middle sections together. Stick the ends of the tape to the top and bottom of the stencil, placing a handle on either side.

Place the stencil on ❷ ▷ the cake and dust with confectioners' sugar or cocoa powder. When you are done, use the tape handles to grasp and lift the stencil straight up and off the cake.

A flourless chocolate cake is rarely frosted, but it can be dressed up a bit with some confectioners' sugar.

Cakes *Decorating*
DUSTING A FLOURLESS CHOCOLATE CAKE

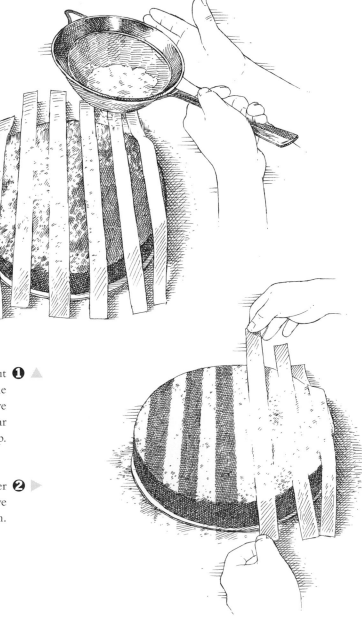

Lay strips of paper about ❶ ▲ ¾ inch wide across the top of the cake, then sieve confectioners' sugar over the top.

Carefully peel away the paper ❷ ▶ strips to reveal an attractive striped pattern.

A glass cake plate with a footed stand and large domed cover is the ideal place to store a frosted cake. Here's how to keep a cake fresh and safe from kitchen accidents if you don't own a cake plate.

Turn the outside bowl of a large salad spinner upside down and place it over the frosted cake, resting the bowl on the edge of the cake plate.

Cakes
IMPROVISING A COVER

Tip 95

The common method for keeping plastic wrap from touching a gooey frosting or glaze is to stick the food with toothpicks and place the wrap over the tooth-picks. Occasionally, though, the sharp points of the toothpicks puncture the wrap, which can then slide down and stick to the frosting. To keep the wrap securely above the frosting, try this method.

Cakes
TRANSPORTING A FROSTED CAKE

❶ Place a miniature marshmallow over the point of each toothpick.

❷ Insert toothpicks into the cake with the marshmallows facing up. Lay the plastic wrap over the marshmallows.

Can Opener
CLEANING

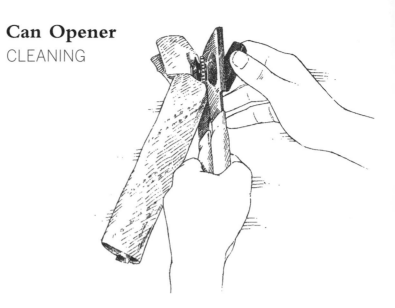

A manual can opener should be cleaned after each use. Running it through the dishwasher accomplishes the task, but usually leaves some rust. Try this quick and easy method instead.

Run a folded sheet of paper towel through the opener. The towel does a great job of cleaning both the blade and the gear.

Cappuccino
FOAMING MILK

Tip 97

Here's how to make steamed, frothy milk for coffee without an expensive espresso machine.

Place a pan filled with heated milk on a potholder or other protective surface and beat the milk with a hand-held electric mixer until the consistency of the milk is foamy and velvety. Milk foamed this way will hold soft peaks, even when spooned into coffee mugs.

Carrots

CUTTING INTO JULIENNE

The term *julienne,* which usually applies to vegetables, means to cut into long, thin strips. It can be tricky to figure out how to julienne long, thin vegetables such as carrots, zucchini, or parsnips.

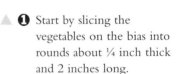

❶ Start by slicing the vegetables on the bias into rounds about ¼ inch thick and 2 inches long.

❷ Fan out several rounds and cut them into ¼ inch strips. This shape is sometimes called the matchstick cut.

Cauliflower
CUTTING INTO FLORETS

Here's an easy way to cut a head of cauliflower into neat florets. Start by pulling off and discarding the outer leaves.

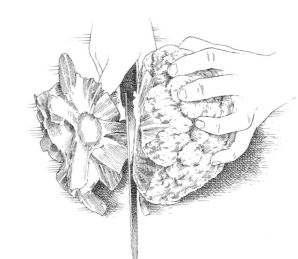

Turn the cauliflower on its **❶** side and cut off the stem near the base of the head with a chef's knife.

Turn the cauliflower so the **❷** stem end is facing up. Using a small chef's knife or large paring knife, cut around the core to remove it.

Separate the individual florets **❸** from the inner stem using the tip of a chef's knife. Cut the florets in half or in quarters, as necessary, to yield pieces of the desired size.

Celery
CHOPPING QUICKLY

Recipes often call for a small amount of chopped celery. Rather than breaking off one or more ribs and ending up with too much, try this method.

With a chef's knife, chop the entire bunch across the top. It is easier to get just the amount you need, and the whole bunch gets shorter as you use it, so it's easier to store.

Celery Root
REMOVING THE THICK PEEL

Tip 101

Celery root is covered with a thick, hairy skin that can't be removed with a vegetable peeler. Because the round root is too large to hold in your hand, using a paring knife can be tricky. Here's how to cut away the peel safely.

Cut off about ½ inch from each end of the celery root so that it can rest flat on a cutting board. To peel, simply cut from top to bottom, rotating the celery root as you remove wide strips of skin.

Cheese

CUTTING HARD CHEESE SAFELY

Tip 102

Because hard cheese is difficult to cut through, many cooks often place one hand over the top of their chef's knife blade and the other over the handle to put their weight into the cut, but a slip could result in an accident. We advise taking this extra safety measure.

Put a folded dish towel between your hand and the blade. This protects your hand and makes the cutting more comfortable.

Tip 103

To achieve paper-thin slices of Parmesan, which make a nice addition to salads, employ your vegetable peeler.

Run a vegetable peeler over a block of Parmesan. Use a light touch for thin shavings.

Cheese

SHAVING PARMESAN

It can be a bother to rewrap goat cheese every time you remove a small portion. Keep goat cheese at the ready with this convenient storage method.

A covered butter dish works well to keep goat cheese neatly protected and easy to use.

Cheese
STORING GOAT CHEESE

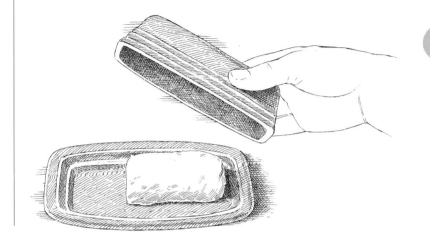

Cheese
SLICING GOAT CHEESE

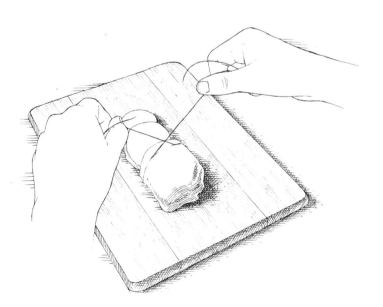

A knife quickly becomes covered with this soft cheese, making it difficult to cut clean, neat slices. Here's how to avoid a sticky situation.

Slide an 18-inch piece of dental floss under a log of goat cheese. Cross the ends of the floss above the cheese and then pull the floss through the cheese to make slices. Move the floss and cut again to make slices of the desired thickness.

Cheese
SHREDDING IN THE FOOD PROCESSOR

It's easy to shred semisoft cheeses such as mozzarella or cheddar in the food processor—until, of course, a big chunk sticks in the feed tube or gums up the shredding disk. Avoid problem stickiness with this trick.

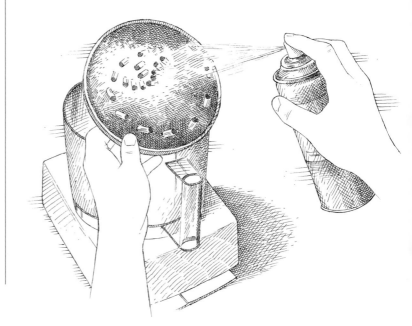

Spray the feed tube, disk, and workbowl of the food processor with a light coating of nonstick cooking spray before you begin shredding.

Cheese
SHREDDING SEMISOFT CHEESE NEATLY

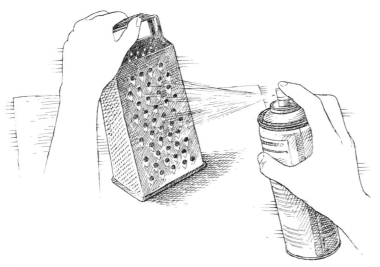

Semisoft cheeses such as cheddar or commercial mozzarella can stick to a box grater and cause a real mess. Here's how to keep the holes on the grater from becoming clogged.

Use nonstick cooking spray to lightly coat the coarse side of the box grater, then shred the cheese as usual. The cooking spray will keep cheese from sticking to the surface of the grater.

Cheese
SLICING FRESH MOZZARELLA

Fresh mozzarella cheese is quite soft, which makes it difficult to slice neatly with a knife. Here's a neater, faster way to slice fresh mozzarella.

❶ Place a piece of mozzarella in an egg slicer. Close the egg slicer to cut through the cheese.

Remove the cheese **❷** from the egg slicer and separate the individual slices.

Cherries
PITTING THREE WAYS

Cherry pitters work well, but not every cook has one on hand. Here are some techniques you can use to pit cherries without a specialized tool. Always work over a bowl to catch the juices.

 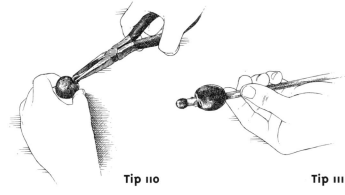

Tip 109

Push the cherry firmly down onto the pointed, jagged end of a pastry bag tip. Take care not to cut your fingers on the points as they pierce the fruit.

Tip 110

Pierce the skin at the stem end with a pair of clean needle-nose pliers. Spread the pliers just enough to grasp the pit, then pull it straight out.

Tip 111

Push a drinking straw through the bottom of the cherry, forcing the pit up and out through the stem end.

Tip 112

Raw chicken is slippery, which means that halving whole breasts can be a hazardous job. This method ensures a firm grip.

Use a folded wad of paper towels to hold the chicken in place as you cut. You can also use a paper towel to firmly grasp chicken skin when removing it from the meat.

Chicken
GETTING A GRIP ON RAW CHICKEN

Chicken
CONTAINING RAW CHICKEN

The possibility of raw chicken contaminating any surface it touches is a real concern. It can be especially tricky to avoid cross-contamination when washing and drying raw chicken. The slippery chicken can slide right off a cutting board onto the counter or soak through protective layers of paper towel. Here's a good way to keep the bird contained as you wash and dry it.

Set the raw chicken in a metal colander while washing it, then pat the chicken dry while it's still in the colander. When done, simply transfer the chicken to your cooking vessel. Remember to wash your hands and the colander with hot, soapy water.

Chicken
SAFELY SEASONING RAW CHICKEN

Tip 114

Many recipes call for seasoning raw chicken with salt and pepper before it is cooked. Touching other dishes or the pepper mill after you've handled raw chicken is a concern if you want to minimize the chances of cross-contamination.

Before handling the chicken, mix the necessary salt and pepper in a small bowl so you can move between the seasoning and chicken without fear of contamination. Discard leftover seasoning mix.

Chicken
SEASONING WITH LEMON

Tip 115

The flavor of lemon is lovely with poultry, but squeezing a lemon half or pouring lemon juice into the cavity of a bird can result in a messy spill. Here's how to limit the mess and maximize the amount of lemon juice that gets into the bird.

Choose a thin-skinned lemon. Cut the lemon in half and turn the halves inside out. It's now easy to rub the cavity evenly and neatly with lemon juice.

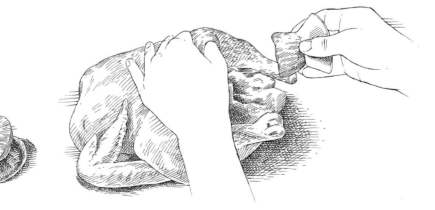

Chicken
BUTTERFLYING FOR FASTER COOKING

Tip 116

A whole small chicken takes an hour or more to roast. If you are in a hurry, you can butterfly the chicken (basically, opening up the bird so it forms a single, flat piece of meat) to shave at least 20 minutes off the cooking time. A butterflied chicken can also be grilled or broiled.

❶ With poultry shears, cut through the bones on either side of the backbone, then remove and discard the backbone.

❷ Turn the chicken over and use the heel of your hand to flatten the breastbone.

Chicken
MAKESHIFT VERTICAL ROASTER

Tip 117

Roasting a chicken on a vertical roaster cuts cooking time significantly and eliminates the need to turn the bird, but some households may not have one.

A tube pan insert mimics a vertical roaster very well. Just place it in a shallow baking dish and spray it with nonstick cooking spray before putting the chicken onto the tube.

Tip 118

Butterflied chicken on the grill cooks faster and more evenly when weighted down.

To weight a butterflied chicken while it grills, set a rimmed baking sheet on top of the chicken. Put two bricks in the pan to add the necessary weight.

Chicken
GRILLING BUTTERFLIED CHICKEN

Chicken
MEASURING THE INTERNAL TEMPERATURE

The most accurate way to tell if a chicken is done is to use an instant-read thermometer. Be sure to put the thermometer into the thickest part of the bird and avoid all bones, which can throw off your reading.

❶ To take the temperature of the thigh, insert the thermometer at an angle into the area between the drumstick and breast. Dark meat should be cooked to 165 or 170 degrees.

❷ To take the temperature of the breast, insert the thermometer from the neck end, holding it parallel to the bird. The breast meat is done at 160 degrees and will begin to dry out at higher temperatures.

Chicken *Cutlets*
TRIMMING FAT AND TENDONS

Tip 120

Boneless, skinless chicken cutlets are a great convenience food. For the best results, take a few minutes to cut away excess fat and tendons that would be unpleasant to eat.

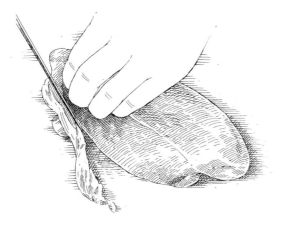

Lay each cutlet tenderloin-❶ side down (the tenderloin is that floppy, thin piece of meat attached to the breast), and smooth the top with your fingers. Any yellow fat will slide to the periphery, where it can be trimmed with a knife.

To remove the tough, white ❷ tendon, turn the cutlet tenderloin-side up, then peel back the thick half of the tenderloin so it lies top down on the work surface. Use the point of a paring knife to cut around the tip of the tendon to expose it, then scrape the tendon free with the knife.

Chicken *Cutlets*
POUNDING CUTLETS

For breaded cutlets, it's important to pound the meat thin. The thicker the cutlet, the more time it needs in the pan, and the more time it spends in the pan, the more likely the breading will burn. The problem is that by the time you get thick cutlets thin enough, they may be so large they won't fit in a skillet. Here's how to minimize the pounding to produce good-looking cutlets that are thin but not excessively large.

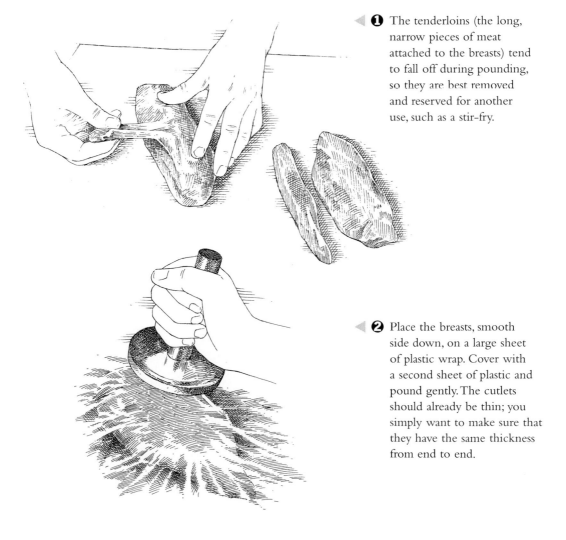

❶ The tenderloins (the long, narrow pieces of meat attached to the breasts) tend to fall off during pounding, so they are best removed and reserved for another use, such as a stir-fry.

❷ Place the breasts, smooth side down, on a large sheet of plastic wrap. Cover with a second sheet of plastic and pound gently. The cutlets should already be thin; you simply want to make sure that they have the same thickness from end to end.

Chicken *Cutlets*
MESS-FREE BREADING

Dipping pounded cutlets into a bowl of beaten eggs and then bread crumbs can be messy. Before you know it, your fingers—not the cutlets—are coated with crumbs. This tip works equally well with turkey or veal cutlets, or fish fillets, such as flounder.

❶ Use a pair of tongs to dip a cutlet into the bowl with the beaten eggs.

❷ Use the tongs to transfer the cutlet to a pie plate filled with bread crumbs. Press the crumbs lightly onto the cutlet with your fingertips to ensure that the crumbs adhere to the surface of the food. Because your fingers were never in the bowl with the eggs, they should remain dry and crumb-free.

Chicken *Cutlets*
KEEPING BREADING FIRMLY ATTACHED

Tip 123

It's disappointing when breading comes off cutlets when they are cooked. Here's how to prevent this from happening with chicken, veal, or turkey cutlets.

Transfer the breaded cutlets to a baking rack set over a baking sheet. Allow the cutlets to dry for 5 minutes. This brief drying time stabilizes the coating so that it won't stick to the pan or fall off.

Chicken *Cutlets*
SAUTÉING SAFELY

Tip 124

Hot fat can splash hands and arms when cold cutlets are added to a skillet. Here's how to minimize that risk.

Lay the cutlet into the pan thick side first. Hang onto the tapered end until the whole cutlet is in the pan. The tapered ends of the cutlets should be at the edges of the pan where the heat is less intense, so they will cook a bit more slowly than the thick middle portions.

Chicken *Cutlets*
CUTTING INTO UNIFORM PIECES

Tip 125

When stir-frying or making pot pies, it's nice to have uniform pieces of chicken breast that will cook at the same rate. Here's how to turn an ungainly cutlet into neat, even strips of meat. It's easiest to slice the cutlet when it has been partially frozen for an hour or so.

Separate the tenderloins ❶ ▲ (the long, floppy pieces of meat) from the breasts and set them aside.

Slice the breasts across ❷ ▲ the grain into long, thin strips. Center pieces need to be cut in half so that they are approximately the same length as end pieces.

Cut the tenderloins on ❸ ▶ the diagonal to produce pieces the same size as the strips of breast meat.

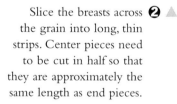

Chicken *Kebabs*
SKEWERING THE MEAT

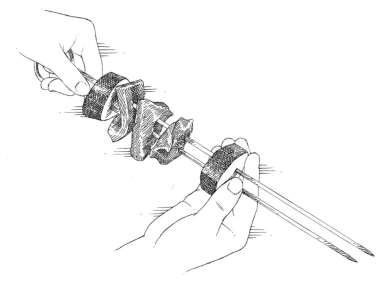

Tip 126

When it comes to kebabs, raw chicken (which is slippery and made more so by the addition of marinade) tends to spin around on the skewer, inhibiting even cooking. Threading the chicken onto two skewers held side by side keeps the chicken stable.

Use one hand to hold two skewers about ½ inch apart, then thread boneless chunks of chicken breast or thigh and vegetables, if desired, onto the skewers simultaneously.

Tip 127

Whole legs are readily available and inexpensive, but they can be difficult to cook and eat. Here's how to separate them neatly.

Chicken *Parts*
SEPARATING THE THIGH FROM THE DRUMSTICK

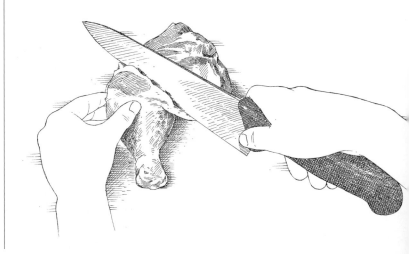

A thin joint connects the drumstick to the thigh. A line of fat runs right over the joint. Simply turn the leg skin-side down and locate the line of fat. With a large chef's knife, cut down through the fat and the joint that lies below to separate the two pieces.

Tip 128

Some cooks love inexpensive chicken wings and buy them especially for grilling or roasting. Yet even wing lovers will admit that eating this jointed piece of chicken can be messy. To minimize the mess, we like to separate the three sections of the wing before cooking.

Chicken *Parts*
TRIMMING WINGS

▲ **❶** With a chef's knife, cut into the skin between the two larger sections of the wing until you hit the joint.

▲ **❷** Bend back the two sections to pop and break the joint.

▲ **❸** Cut through the skin and flesh to completely separate the two meaty portions. One portion will contain the thin wingtip, which has absolutely no meat. Hack off the wingtip and either discard or save it for stock. The two remaining pieces are small enough to be eaten as finger food and much less awkward to hold.

Chicken *Parts*
GRILLING BONE-IN BREASTS

Tip 129

Everyone loves grilled bone-in, skin-on breasts. But all too often the exterior burns before the meat in thick breasts is fully cooked. Here's how to make sure the meat near the bone is done without causing the skin to burn. You can use this same trick to finish cooking thick chops.

Once the chicken is nicely browned and nearly done, slide the pieces to a cool part of the grill and cover them with a disposable aluminum roasting pan. The pan traps the heat to create an oven-like effect on your grill. While the meat continues to cook, the skin won't color any further.

Chiles

FREEZING CHIPOTLE CHILES IN ADOBO SAUCE

Chipotles (smoked, dried jalapeño chiles) are among our favorite chiles because they are so flavorful. Chipotles are often packed in adobo sauce (a vinegary tomato sauce flavored with garlic) and canned. Because a little bit of chipotle chile goes a long way, it can be difficult to use up an entire can once it has been opened. Rather than letting the remaining chiles go bad in the refrigerator, try this trick. We like to preserve tomato paste in the same fashion.

❶ Spoon out the chipotles, each with a couple of teaspoons of adobo sauce, onto different areas of a cookie sheet lined with parchment or waxed paper. Place the cookie sheet in the freezer.

❷ Once frozen, the chipotles should be transferred to a zipper-lock plastic bag and stored in the freezer. You can remove them, one at a time, as needed. They will keep indefinitely.

A microwave set at 50 percent power is a great place to melt chocolate, but not everyone has a microwave. Here's an equally simple and ingenious tip. Whatever you do, don't melt plain chocolate directly on the stovetop. The heat is too intense, and the chocolate will likely burn.

Chocolate
MELTING IN A DRIP COFFEE MACHINE

Roughly chop the chocolate and place it in a small, heatproof bowl. Cover the top of the bowl with plastic wrap, being careful not to bring the plastic too far down the sides of the bowl. Place the bowl on the burner plate of an electric drip coffee machine, turn on the coffee maker, and let the gentle heat of the burner melt the chocolate without scorching it.

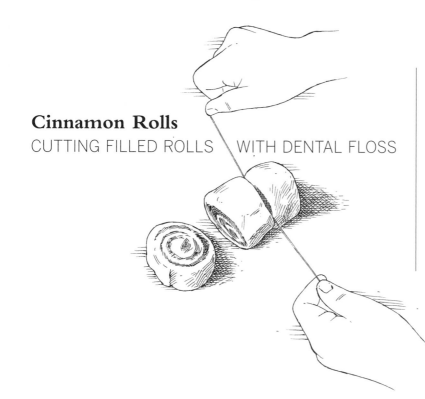

Cinnamon Rolls
CUTTING FILLED ROLLS WITH DENTAL FLOSS

A knife can squish and tear soft yeast doughs, causing the filling to leak out the sides. Here's how to cut the dough for cinnamon rolls quickly and safely.

Hold a piece of dental floss in each hand and carefully saw through the dough with the floss to separate individual pieces.

Clams
SCRUBBING WITH A BRUSH

Many recipes instruct the cook to scrub clams and other shellfish. Don't skip this step; many clams and mussels have bits of sand embedded in the shell that can mar a sauce.

Use a soft brush, sometimes sold in kitchen shops as a vegetable brush, to scrub clams under cold, running water.

Clams
STRAINING PRECIOUS LIQUID

Tip 134

Clams (as well as mussels) are often steamed with a little wine and herbs in a covered pot. The cooking liquid is delicious but sometimes gritty. Here's how to remove the grit. (Note that bits of garlic, shallots, and herbs will be lost when the liquid is strained, but their flavors remain in the liquid.)

Pour the cooking liquid through a sieve lined with a single paper towel and set over a measuring cup.

Cocktails *Gibson*
QUICK CHILLING

Here's a novel way to chill a Gibson (a martini garnished with onions instead of olives) without diluting your drink with ice.

Use frozen pearl onions to garnish your Gibson instead of the traditional pickled onions.

Cocktails
MAKESHIFT MARTINI SHAKER

Cocktails like martinis and Manhattans should be shaken, not stirred, and not just because James Bond says so. Shaking the cocktail with the ice chills the mixture more thoroughly than simply stirring it. If your bar isn't equipped with a proper cocktail shaker, try this.

A spill-proof coffee mug with a screw-on lid makes a fine substitute. Just be sure to place your finger over the sipping hole when you shake. The lid will keep the ice in the "shaker" when you pour.

Coffee
EFFICIENT GRINDING

Many inexpensive blade-type grinders grind coffee beans unevenly, producing some powder as well as some larger pieces of bean. Here's how to even out the grind.

With your hand over the hopper, lift the whole unit off the counter and shake it gently as it grinds. (The motion is akin to blending a martini in a cocktail shaker.) By moving the beans around, you help the machine grind more evenly.

When using a manual drip coffee maker, the grounds can spill down into the pot if the paper filter folds over on itself when the water is poured into it. To avoid this problem, try this simple method.

Barely dampen the paper filter with water and press it against the sides of the plastic cone. When you add the coffee and pour the water, the filter will adhere to the cone.

Coffee
STABILIZING COFFEE FILTERS

Coffee Cakes
DRIZZLING WITH WHITE ICING

The lines of white icing that adorn many coffee cakes are nothing more than sifted confectioners' sugar thinned with a little milk and flavored with a splash of vanilla. Here's how to drizzle the icing over a cooled coffee cake in nice thin lines. Use this tip to decorate molasses spice cookies, too.

Dip a large dinner spoon into the bowl with the icing. Quickly move the spoon back and forth over the coffee cake, letting the icing fall in thin ribbons from the end of the spoon. Keep dipping the spoon back into the bowl of icing until the coffee cake is amply iced.

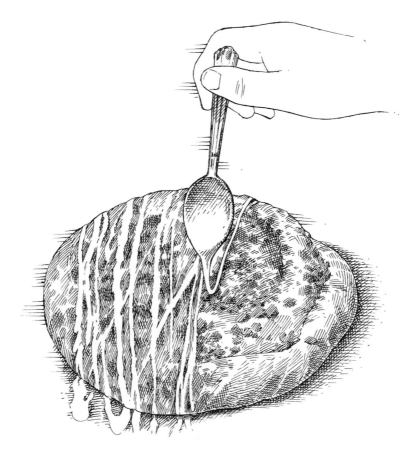

Colander
IMPROVISING WITH STEAMER BASKET

If you are short on colanders, you might try this handy substitute.

Use a steamer basket to drain vegetables, pasta, and the like. Just be sure to pour slowly and carefully because the sides are not as high as the sides of a regular colander.

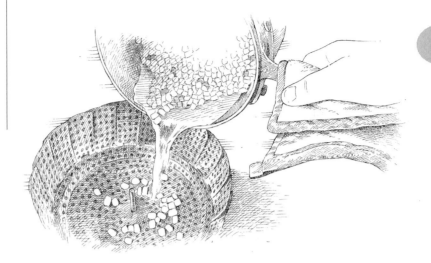

Cookies
DISTRIBUTING GOODIES EVENLY IN DOUGH

Tip 141

The last few cookies from a batch of chocolate chip cookies never seem to have as many chips as the first few cookies. The same thing often happens with nuts and raisins. Here's how to avoid this common problem.

Reserve some of the chips, nuts, or other goodies and mix them into the dough after about half of it has been scooped out for cookies. This way, the last of the cookies will have as much good stuff as the first batch.

For the best-looking cookies, it is important to start with balls of dough that are all the same size. Many recipes suggest rolling the dough into balls of a specific diameter, but it's difficult to measure the balls with a ruler set on the counter. Here's how to get an accurate measurement.

Cookies
MAKING EVEN-SIZED BALLS OF DOUGH

Set the ruler on top of the bowl. Rather than placing the ball of dough on top of the ruler (where it's hard to measure the equator), bring the ball up along the side of the ruler.

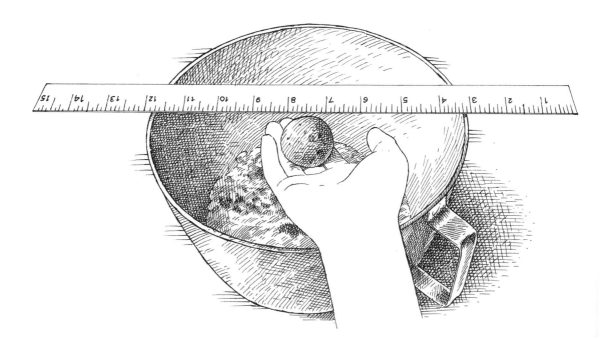

Cookies
MEASURING OUT STICKY DOUGH

Some cookie dough can be so sticky that your hands become a mess in no time. Here's a way to get equal-sized balls of dough without soiling your hands.

Use a small ice cream scoop to measure out the dough. Dip the scoop into cold water between scoopings to ensure that the dough releases easily every time.

Cookies
KEEPING SEPARATE AS THEY BAKE

Many types of cookies can spread into each other on the cookie sheet as they bake, resulting in odd shapes and soft edges. To keep the cookies separate, try this method of arranging the dough balls.

Instead of placing the dough balls in neat rows of three or four so that all the cookies line up, alternate the rows. For example, three cookies in the first row, two in the second, three in the third, two in the fourth, and so on.

Cookies
FREEZING DOUGH

Keeping frozen dough on hand means you can bake just as many, or as few, cookies as you like without first having to whip up a batch of dough. Most cookie doughs can withstand a month or so in the freezer.

Form the dough into balls and arrange them on a cookie sheet lined with parchment or waxed paper. Place the cookie sheet in the freezer. When the balls of dough are frozen, place them in a zipper-lock plastic bag or small airtight container. When you want to make cookies, remove as many balls as you like and bake as directed, increasing the cooking time by a minute or two.

Cookies
SLICING ICEBOX COOKIES

Logs of dough stored in the freezer are great to have on hand, but we've noticed that the dough can soften by the time you get to the end, making it difficult to cut neat slices. Here's how to prevent this problem.

Cookies
ROTATING BAKING SHEETS

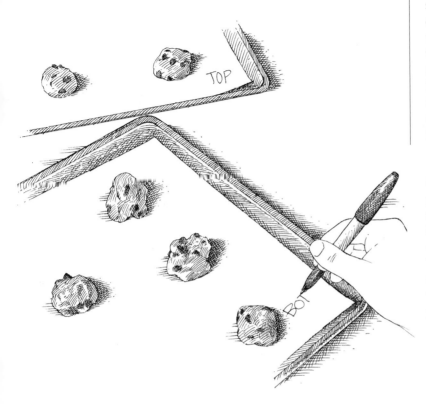

Often when you have two sheets of cookies in the oven at once, the recipe will direct you to reverse them from front to back and top to bottom. In the bustle of a busy kitchen, however, it can be a challenge to keep track of the direction of the pans.

Line the cookie sheets with parchment paper and mark the front edge of the paper, indicating which pans start on the top and the bottom. This will help you keep track of which edge goes where when you reverse the pans' positions.

❶ Remove the dough log from the freezer and cut it into pieces no more than 3 inches long. Place all but one piece of dough back in the freezer.

Using a very sharp chef's knife, slice the piece **❷** of dough left out. To prevent one side of the log from flattening due to the pressure you put on it, roll the dough one-eighth of a turn after every slice. Once this first piece of dough has been completely sliced, retrieve the next piece from the freezer and slice in the same manner.

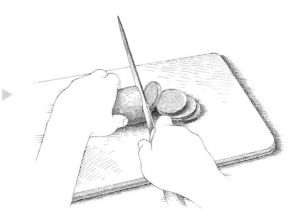

Cookies
REUSING THE SAME BAKING SHEET

Baking batch after batch of cookies can be a frustrating exercise, especially when you have only one cookie sheet. No one wants to scrub the same baking sheet many times, but dough balls must be placed on a clean surface. Here's how to work quickly and efficiently when you have just one cookie sheet.

❶ Load up a sheet of parchment paper with balls of dough, slide the paper onto the cookie sheet, and place the cookies in the oven.

While the first batch is baking, load up a second ❷ ▶ piece of parchment paper with balls of dough.

When the baked cookies ❸ ▼ come out of the oven, whisk the parchment and its cargo onto a cooling rack. After cooling the baking sheet with a quick rinse and dry, it's ready for the next prepared batch.

Cookies
SHAPING THUMBPRINTS

The best thumbprints have a deep, round indentation to hold the dollop of jam or chocolate securely. Your thumb can be used to make a deep indentation, but for perfectly round ones, try this.

Press the back side of a melon baller into dough balls before baking. The end of a wooden honey dipper is also well suited to this task.

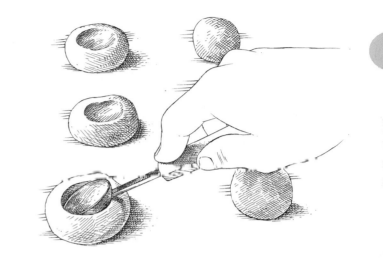

Cookies
SHAPING SUGAR COOKIES

Sugar cookies should have an even thickness from side to side and they must be lightly coated with granulated sugar. Here's how to accomplish both goals with one motion.

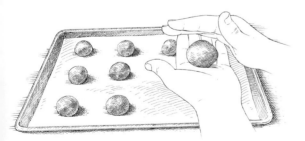

❶ Roll a piece of dough between your palms into a ball (about 1½ tablespoons of dough formed into a ball about 1½ inches in diameter). Roll the ball of dough in a bowl filled with granulated sugar.

❷ Choose a drinking glass that measures about 2 inches across its bottom. Butter the bottom of the glass and dip it into a bowl of sugar. Use the glass to flatten the dough balls, dipping the glass back into the sugar after shaping every other cookie.

Cookies
SHAPING LACE COOKIES INTO CUPS

Lifting lace cookies off the pan and shaping them before they harden and become brittle requires exact timing. The method we use makes it easy to lift the cookies while still hot. It also eliminates the need to move the hot cookies off the baking sheet with a spatula, a process that often results in torn or bunched-up cookies.

Line up four upside-down ramekins or small bowls. ❶ ▽
Cut a sheet of parchment paper to fit the baking pan, then cut that sheet into four equal pieces.

When the cookies come out of ❸ the oven, remove one of the parchment squares from the sheet to a plate to cool, leaving the others on the hot pan to keep them warm and pliable. Cool the cookie on the plate to the right consistency for molding (30 to 60 seconds).

▽ ❷ Drop one tablespoon of batter onto the center of each piece of parchment and bake.

❹ Lift the parchment square, turn the cookie over, and place it on the bottom of the ramekin or bowl to shape it. Lift the parchment from the cookie. Repeat steps 3 and 4 with the other cookies. Cool the cookies before lifting them off the ramekins or bowls.

Tip 152

When baking lots of cookies, as for the holidays, it's inevitable that some of the cookies will end up overbrowned or even burnt in some spots. This cookie-saving tip works well with lightly singed cookies, but not thoroughly burnt ones.

Gently grate the burnt layer off the bottoms with a Microplane grater/zester.

Cookies
RESCUING BURNT COOKIES

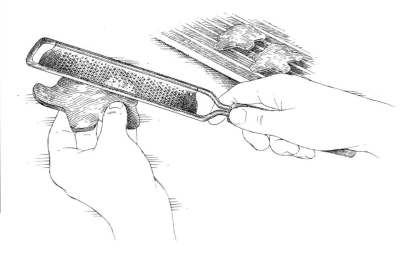

Almond crescents as well as butterballs or Mexican wedding cakes should have a thick, even coating of confectioners' sugar. Many recipes suggest sugaring the cookies as soon as they come out of the oven. Although the coating adheres well to warm cookies, the sugar often tastes pasty because it has melted a bit. Here's how to ensure that the coating is thick but never pasty.

Cookies
SUGARING CRESCENT COOKIES

Once the cookies have cooled, roll them in a bowl of confectioners' sugar and shake off the excess. Don't worry if the coating is spotty in places; just go ahead and store the cookies in an airtight container. When ready to serve, roll the cookies in sugar again to cover any bare spots.

Cookies

MAKING YOUR OWN COLORED SUGAR

Tip 154

Colored sugar makes a fine decoration for holiday cookies. However, many stores carry just one or two colors, and you often end up with leftover sugar. Here's how to customize your colors and make only as much as you need.

❶ Sprinkle about ½ cup granulated sugar evenly over the bottom of a pie plate or metal bowl. Add about five drops of food coloring and mix thoroughly.

To be sure the color is evenly **❷** distributed, push the sugar through a fine sieve. Spread the sugar back on the pie plate or on a baking sheet and let dry completely.

Cookies
ORGANIZING COOKIE DECORATIONS

During the holiday season you may be decorating cookies several times. Here's a good way to organize your favorite decorations. If you bake with children, you'll also appreciate this neat way to organize colored sugar, sprinkles, and such.

Place a different decoration in each cup of a muffin tin, which is easy to move around the kitchen and store for next time.

Cookies
EASY DRYING FOR FROSTED COOKIES

A box or tin of colorful frosted cookies makes a nice gift to friends and neighbors, especially around the holidays. But before the cookies can be wrapped, the frosting has to dry thoroughly, and it can be a real challenge to find enough space to spread out a few dozen cookies in a cramped kitchen.

Coat the rim of a small paper **❶** cup with frosting and invert on the middle of a paper plate. Arrange as many drying cookies around the cup as will fit comfortably on the plate. Dab the exposed rim of the cup with frosting, then make another plate in the same manner and stack it on top of the first.

Repeat until you have **❷** a stack of four or five cookie-laden plates.

Cookies
KEEPING FRESH

Decorative cookie jars, like those made from ceramic, are convenient and attractive but not airtight, allowing fresh-baked cookies to go stale quickly. This method preserves the cookies' freshness and allows you to keep the pretty jar.

Line the inside of the jar with a large plastic zipper-lock bag, place the cookies in the bag, and seal tightly.

Cooking Fat
EASY DISPOSAL

Excess fat from cooked bacon, sausage, or ground meat can clog kitchen sink pipes. Here's an easy way to get rid of this fat.

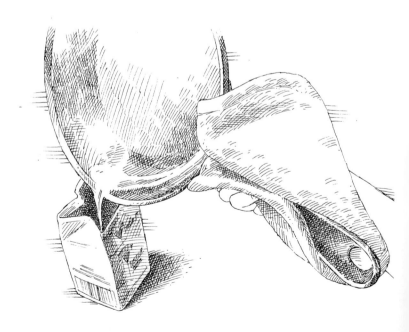

Wash out empty heavy-duty cardboard containers from half-and-half or heavy cream and save them under the sink. When you have some hot bacon or other fat to throw away, pull out one of the stored cartons and pour it in. Once the fat has cooled, close the carton and dispose of it.

Cooking Spray
NO-MESS SPRAYING

Many cooks have had to clean up the oily film on their counter or workspace that results from using an aerosol nonstick cooking spray. Here's how to avoid this problem.

Open the dishwasher door, place the item to be greased right on the door, and spray away. Any excess or overspray will be cleaned off the door the next time you run the dishwasher.

Cookware
PROTECTING NONSTICK PANS

The surfaces on nonstick pans can chip or scratch easily, especially if you stack pans in a cabinet. Here are two ways to store them efficiently and safely.

Tip 160

Place a doubled sheet of paper towel or bubble wrap between each pan as you nest the pans in a stack.

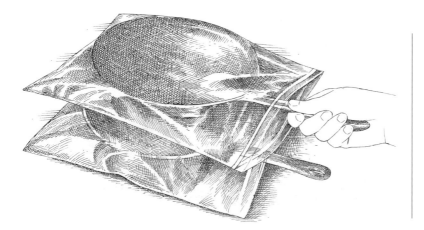

Tip 161

Before stacking the pans, slide them into large plastic zipper-lock bags (the 2-gallon size for 10-inch pans and the 1-gallon size for 8-inch pans). The plastic will protect the nonstick surface.

KEEPING TRACK OF POT LIDS

Most cooks throw all their lids into one
drawer, making it hard to match the right lid with the right pan.
Here are a few ways to keep your lids organized.

Tip 162

If you store your pans in a drawer, install a slender expansion curtain rod in the front of the pot drawer. Stand the lids up straight against the rod, which will keep the lids in sight and reach.

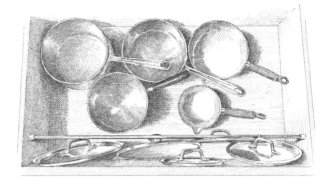

Tip 163

If you store your pans in a cabinet, set an adjustable V-rack for roasting to the widest setting, then stand the lids up in the slots between the wires of the rack.

Tip 164

If you hang your pans from hooks, slide the loop handle of the lid right onto the handle of its matching pan, then hang the pan from the hook.

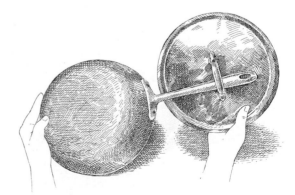

Rather than burning
your fingers or searching
around for a potholder
every time you want to
lift a lid off a pot on the
stove, try this tip.

Before cooking, wedge a
wine cork under the handle
of the lid. The cork stays cool
when the lid gets hot, giving
you something safe to grab
onto when lifting the lid.

Cookware
LIFTING HOT LIDS

Cookware
CLEANING POTS AND PANS

Pans containing baked-on
coatings of burned cheese
or sauce from a macaroni
and cheese, lasagna, or
fondue dish pose a
formidable cleaning task.

Cover the burned-on mess
with dishwashing soap and
a small amount of boiling
water. Allow it to rest
overnight. The next
morning the mess
washes away with ease.

Cookware
CLEANING COPPER

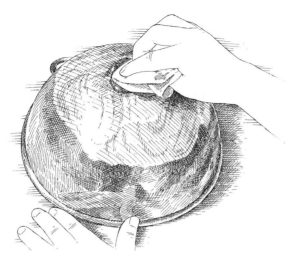

Copper cookware looks great but is notorious for tarnishing quickly. Commercial copper polish requires some scrubbing and costs a lot of money. Here's a way to save money and work.

With a paper towel, smear a thin layer of ketchup over the tarnished surface. Wait 5 minutes, then wipe and rinse off the ketchup. The acidity in the ketchup lifts the tarnish away.

Tip 168

Cooks often find themselves without enough cooling racks, especially during the holidays when baking lots of pies. Jury-rig extra racks with this method.

Cooling Rack
IMPROVISING WITH DINNER KNIVES

Place four dinner knives on a countertop, alternating the direction of the blades and spacing them more than an inch apart. The knives will provide a stable, elevated surface.

Corn
DRAINING HOT BOILED CORN

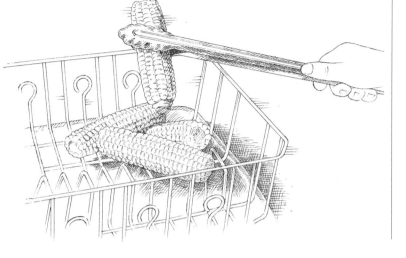

Tip 169

Hot boiled corn cobs are awkward to drain in a conventional colander.

Drain hot boiled corn in a clean dish rack, which can easily accommodate the bulky cobs.

Tip 170

Cutting the kernels from long ears of corn can be tricky. Tapered ears wobble on cutting boards, and kernels can go flying around the kitchen. Here's a way to work safely and more neatly.

Cut the ear in half crosswise and then stand the half ears on their cut surfaces, which are flat and stable.

Corn
REMOVING THE KERNELS

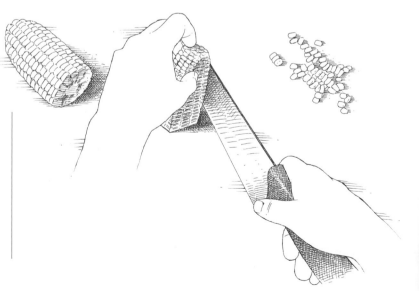

Corn

BUTTERING CORN AND BREAD TOGETHER

Using a knife to butter an ear of corn can be messy and frustrating, as the melting butter slides off the knife and down the ear. Here's an easier way to butter corn.

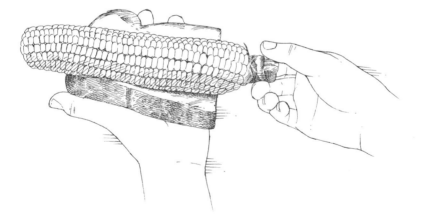

❶ If serving sliced bread with dinner, spread a thick layer of butter on the bread.

❷ Hold the bread in one hand and roll the hot ear of corn over the buttered bread, evenly coating the corn with butter.

Corn
PREPARING CORN FOR GRILLING

Adding flavor from the grill is a nice but tricky thing to do with fresh corn. Husked ears tend to burn, and unhusked ears steam on the grill, failing to pick up that great smoky flavor. Here's how to keep corn from burning while still infusing it with grilled flavor.

Before grilling, remove all but ❶ ▲
the innermost layer of husk.

▼ ❷ Use scissors to snip off the tassel. The ear can then be grilled without soaking or further preparation. When done (see next tip), simply peel back the remaining husk and serve.

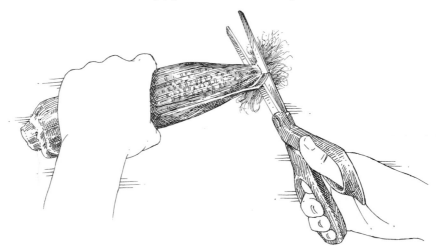

Corn

KNOWING WHEN GRILLED CORN IS DONE

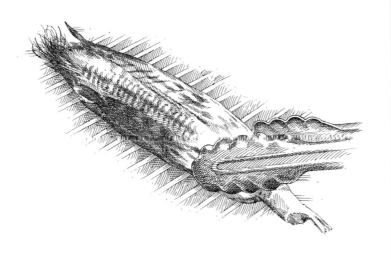

Most cooks know how long they like to cook corn in water. But timing can be tricky when grilling corn because fires vary in intensity. If you prepare corn according to the method outlined in the previous tip, there's a visual clue you can use to judge when the corn is tender.

As soon as the husk picks up the dark silhouette of kernels and begins to pull away from the tip of the ear, the corn is ready to come off the grill.

If you like to grill pieces of corn on the cob kebab-style, you know how difficult it can be to poke the skewer, especially one made from bamboo, through the thick center of the cob. Here's a way to streamline the process.

After cutting the cob into chunks, run a corkscrew through each piece, which will make it easy to run a skewer in. The coiled hole helps ensure a snug fit.

Corn

CORN ON THE KEBAB

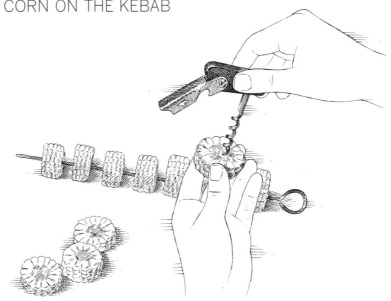

Corn
MILKING

Releasing the milk from corn kernels yields its sweet flavor for use in creamed corn, corn pudding, fritters, and chowder. Milking corn needn't be a time-consuming, cumbersome process.

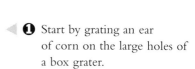

❶ Start by grating an ear of corn on the large holes of a box grater.

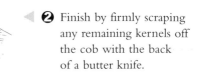

❷ Finish by firmly scraping any remaining kernels off the cob with the back of a butter knife.

Cornish Hens

PRICKING SKIN TO PREVENT BALLOONING

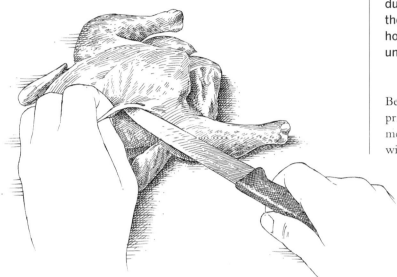

Cornish hens can build up juices beneath the skin during cooking, causing the skin to balloon. Here's how to prevent this unsightly occurrence.

Before cooking, carefully prick the skin (but not the meat) on the breast and leg with the tip of a knife.

Countertop

PROTECTING

On some types of countertops, such as old-fashioned Formica, you run the risk of damaging the surface by setting a hot pan down on it.

Purchase an attractive 12 by 12-inch tile and position it next to your stovetop to use as a trivet. This way, pots coming off of a burner can go onto the trivet, leaving the burner free for another pot.

Crabs
CLEANING SOFT-SHELLS

Although your fishmonger will probably offer to clean soft-shell crabs for you, for optimum freshness you should clean the crabs yourself, right before cooking.

Start by cutting off the ❶ ▶ mouth with kitchen shears; the mouth is the first part of the shell to harden. You can also cut off the eyes at the same time, but this is purely for aesthetic reasons, as the eyes are edible.

◀ ❷ Lift the pointed side of the crab and cut out the spongy off-white gills underneath; the gills are fibrous and watery and unpleasant to eat.

Finally, turn the crab on ❸ ▶ its back and cut off the triangular, or T-shaped, "apron flap" at the tail.

Cream
CHILLING THE BOWL

For the best results, you should chill a bowl before whipping cream in it. For many cooks, the freezer is either too small or too full to accommodate a large bowl. Here's how we accomplish this task.

❶ At least 15 minutes before whipping the cream, fill the bowl with ice cubes and cold water, place the whisk in the ice water (it helps to chill this as well), and put the bowl into the refrigerator.

❷ When ready to whip the cream, dump out the ice water, dry the bowl and whisk, and add the cream. The bowl will stay cold as you work, and the cream whips up beautifully.

Cream

JUDGING WHEN CREAM IS PROPERLY WHIPPED

Many recipes instruct the cook to whip cream to either soft or stiff peaks.
Here are easy ways to tell when you should stop beating.

Tip 180	**Tip 181**
Cream whipped to soft peaks will droop slightly from the ends of the beaters.	Cream whipped to stiff peaks will cling tightly to the ends of the beaters and hold its shape.

Cucumbers

SEEDING

Tip 182

In many recipes, the watery seeds are removed from cucumbers. Here's an easy way to accomplish this task.

Halve the cucumber (already peeled if desired) lengthwise. Run a small spoon inside each cucumber half to scoop out the seeds and surrounding liquid.

Cucumbers
WEIGHTING

Even when seeded, cucumbers can give off a lot of liquid and make dressings too watery. For this reason, we think it's a good idea to salt and weight cucumbers before dressing them.

❶ Place seeded cucumber halves flat-side down on a work surface and slice them on the diagonal into ¼-inch-thick pieces.

Toss the cucumbers with **❷** salt (1 teaspoon for every cucumber) in a colander. To help extract as much liquid as possible, weight the cucumbers. To apply the weight evenly, fill a gallon-sized zipper-lock bag with water and seal tightly. Place the bag over the cucumbers in the colander. Let the cucumbers drain for at least 1 hour, preferably for 3 hours. There's no need to rinse off the salt; just make sure not to add salt to the dressing.

Custards
EASY REMOVAL FROM WATER BATH

Baked custards, like pots de crème and crème brûlée, are cooked in a water bath to ensure slow, even cooking, making it hard to remove the ramekins without burning fingers or marring the surface of the custard with a potholder.

Slip rubber bands around the tips of a pair of tongs. The rubber provides a sure grip for easy removal, and there's no danger of burning fingers.

Cutting Board
KEEPING IT STABLE

Chefs use a no-skid mat beneath a cutting board to keep it from slipping all over the counter. If you don't own a mat, try this tip.

Lay a damp sheet of paper towel on the counter, then put the cutting board on top. The damp paper towel holds the board in place and can be used to wipe down the counter. When you are done, throw the soiled towel out.

Dishwasher – Freezer

Dishwasher
SECURING SMALL ITEMS

It's easy for small kitchen utensils such as cake testers, trussing needles, pastry tips, and measuring spoons to fall through the slots in the dishwasher silverware container. Try this handy tip instead.

❶ Stuff a small nylon pot scrubber into the bottom of the cutlery container.

❷ Secure small items by sticking them into the pot scrubber. The scrubber will prevent anything from falling through.

A little extra care in
loading silverware into
the dishwasher can make
unloading go faster.

Dishwasher
UNLOADING SILVERWARE SIMPLIFIED

When loading the dishwasher,
separate the silverware by
type. At unloading time,
simply grab each bunch
of silverware and store.

Duck
PREPARING FOR GRILLING

Duck breast is great grilled, but its abundant fat can be a problem, causing flare-ups on the grill that result in charred and ruined meat. Removing the skin entirely can cause the meat to dry out. Here's an easy compromise.

❶ With a sharp chef's knife, trim any overhanging skin and fat from around each breast half. Slide your fingers under the remaining skin along the length of the breast to loosen. Turn the breast half on its side and slice off some of the skin and fat so that only a strip of skin (1½ to 2 inches) remains in the center of each breast half.

❷ Using a paring knife, score the skin on each breast half diagonally 3 or 4 times to allow the fat to melt during cooking.

Dumplings
NO-STICK STEAMING

Steamed dumplings often stick to the steamer and tear as you try to remove them. Here's how to prevent this from happening.

Line the steamer basket with sturdy lettuce leaves and then place the dumplings on top of the lettuce. This trick can be used with any steamed pastry item.

Eggplant
SLICING FOR GRILLING

Eggplant is often sliced lengthwise for grilling. The outer pieces are covered with skin and won't get those nice grill marks on both sides unless you use this tip, which also works with zucchini.

Use a sharp knife to remove the peel from the outer eggplant slices. Besides creating more attractive grill marks, we find that the flesh cooks better when directly exposed to the heat of the grill.

A standing mixer is the best tool for whipping egg whites. However, it can be difficult to tell when the eggs are properly whipped. Also, the speed of the mixer means that eggs can go from properly whipped to overwhipped in seconds. Here's an easy way to keep from overbeating egg whites. Use the same technique when whipping cream in a standing mixer.

Eggs
BEATING THE WHITES

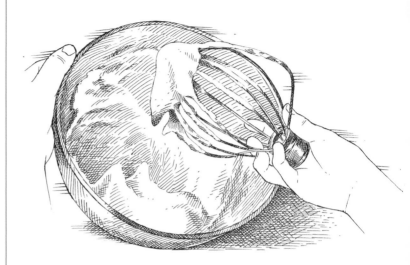

Just before the whites reach the proper consistency, turn off the mixer. Detach the whisk attachment and remove the bowl from the mixer. Use the whisk attachment to make the last few strokes by hand. Be sure to scrape along the bottom of the bowl.

Eggs
FOLDING IN BEATEN WHITES

Recipes for everything from cakes to soufflés call for beaten egg whites, which are usually folded into the batter just before it is baked. If you mix in the whites too vigorously, the cake or soufflé may not rise. If you don't incorporate them thoroughly, you may be left with eggy patches after baking. Here's the best way to fold beaten egg whites into a batter. Start by vigorously stirring a portion of the beaten whites (most recipes will call for a quarter or third of the whites) into the batter. This lightens the texture of the batter so the rest of the whites can be folded in more gently.

❶ Scrape the remaining whites into the bowl. Starting at the top of the bowl, use a rubber spatula to cut through the middle of the whites.

❷ Turn the edge of the spatula toward you so it moves up the sides of the bowl.

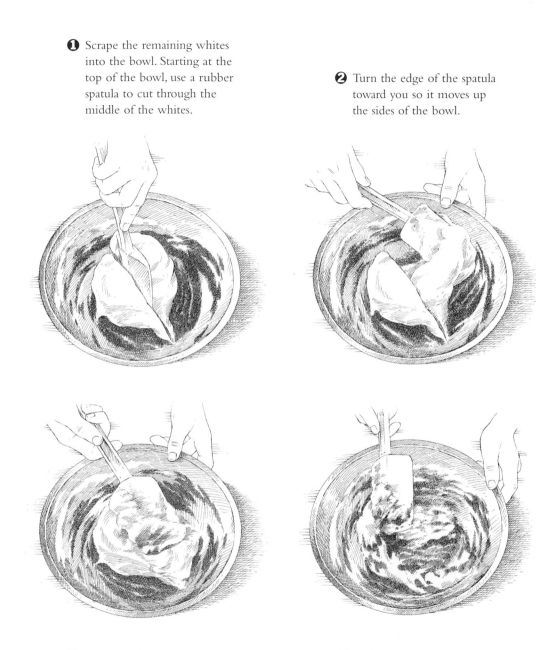

❸ Continue this motion, going full circle, until the spatula is back at the center of the bowl again.

❹ Follow this procedure four more times, turning the bowl a quarter turn each time. Finally, use the spatula to scrape around the entire circumference of the bowl.

Eggs *Deviled*
FLUFFY FILLINGS

A pasty, heavy texture in the yolk filling is the downfall of many deviled eggs.
Here are two ways to keep the filling light and fluffy.

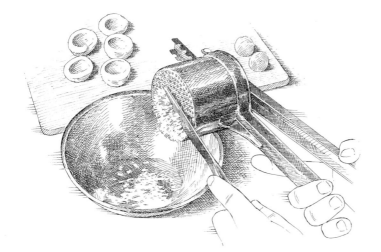

Tip 193

If making many deviled eggs at one time, press the yolks gently through a potato ricer and use a knife to shave the extruded yolk off the bottom of the ricer and into a bowl. The yolks come out smooth, light, and airy.

Tip 194

When making smaller batches, grate the yolks using the drum of a Mouli grater. Don't apply too much pressure on the hopper, and the yolks will emerge light and fluffy.

Once the yolks have been riced or grated and then seasoned, the filling is ready to be piped back into the empty egg halves. A pastry bag fitted with a star tip is the ideal tool for the job. Here's what to do if you don't have a pastry bag.

Eggs *Deviled*
USING A PLASTIC BAG TO FILL EGGS

Spoon the yolk mixture into a plastic bag. Snip a small piece from one bottom corner of the bag, then gently squeeze the filling through the hole into the egg halves.

Eggs *Deviled*

KEEPING FILLED EGGS STABLE FOR TRANSPORT

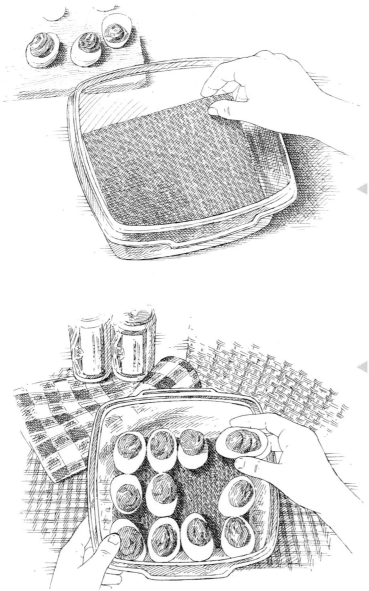

Preparing beautiful deviled eggs requires care, so it goes without saying that you want them to arrive at your destination looking as perfect as they did in your kitchen. Here's how to keep the eggs upright if you want to transport them.

❶ Cut a clean piece of rubberized shelf or drawer liner (available at hardware stores) to the size of the dish that will hold the eggs. Make sure to choose a dish with relatively high sides—a square plastic storage container with a lid is perfect.

❷ Place the fitted liner on the bottom of the container, then stock it with enough eggs to fill it in a single layer. The liner keeps the eggs from sliding when the container is moved.

Eggs *Fried*
GETTING THE EGGS INTO THE SKILLET

Fried eggs cook so quickly that seconds can make the difference between a runny yolk and one that has set. If you add the eggs one at a time to a hot pan, the first egg will be done well before the last. Adding all the eggs at exactly the same time means that all the eggs will be done at the same time.

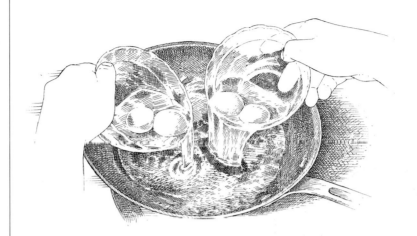

Crack two eggs into each of two small bowls. When the pan is ready, slide the eggs from both bowls into the skillet from opposite sides.

Eggs *Hard-Cooked*
LIFTING SAFELY

We don't like to use a slotted spoon to transfer hard-cooked eggs from the pot, because a poorly timed nudge, shift in balance, or unsteady hand could send the eggs flying out of the spoon and onto the floor.

A pasta server's deep bowl is the ideal size for cradling eggs securely.

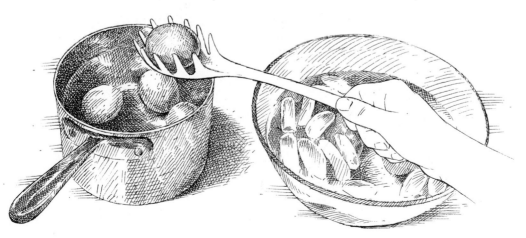

Sometimes it can be difficult to tell which eggs in your refrigerator are raw and which ones are hard-cooked. Here's a simple trick to keep them straight. This works only with white eggs.

Eggs *Hard-Cooked*
IDENTIFYING THEM IN THE REFRIGERATOR

Add a little balsamic vinegar to the cooking water along with the eggs. This dark brown vinegar tints the eggshells so you can distinguish them from bright white raw eggs.

Eggs *Hard-Cooked*
CUBING PERFECTLY

For egg salad and other dishes, it's nice to have perfect cubes. Hard-cooked eggs are slippery and oddly shaped, so many cooks end up with uneven pieces or, worse, pieces that are slightly mashed. Here's a neat trick that's fast and foolproof.

Place the hard-cooked ❶ ▽ egg in the depression of a slicer and cut the egg lengthwise.

▽ ❷ Turn the egg a quarter turn and slice crosswise.

▽ ❸ Rotate the egg 90 degrees, so one end is facing up, and slice from top to bottom.

Eggs *Hard-Cooked*
CRUMBLING EGGS

Tip 201

For garnishes and salads, it is best to use very fine pieces of hard-cooked egg. Chopping the egg can be tricky and usually results in fairly large pieces. Here's a better option.

Press the egg through a mesh sieve to yield fine, even pieces.

Tip 202

As with frying (see tip 197, page 145), it is important to get all the eggs into the pan at the same time when poaching them. Because there's water in the pan, you must use a slightly different method.

Crack each egg into a small cup with a handle. When the water is ready, lower the lips of each cup into the water at the same time and then tip the eggs into the pan.

Eggs *Poached*
GETTING FOUR EGGS INTO THE WATER

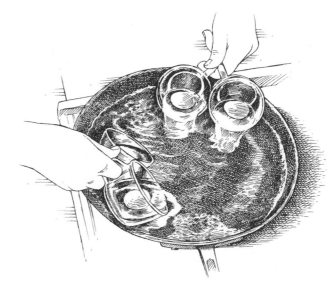

Eggs *Omelet*
FOLDING

Omelets are somewhat delicate and when filled can be especially difficult to fold, then remove from the pan without ripping open. Try this quick and easy way to transfer and fold the omelet simultaneously— minus the rips and tears.

❶ Be sure that the handle of the nonstick pan is facing you, and when the egg is just set and still moist on the surface, immediately fill the omelet by sprinkling the warmed filling onto the left side of the omelet, or if you're left-handed, the right side.

Tip the pan slightly and slide **❷** the filled half of the omelet onto a warm plate. With a slight turn of the wrist, slightly invert the pan so the other side of the omelet folds over the filling.

The bitter flavor of endive softens somewhat when grilled, but keeping the leaves intact and cooking evenly can be a challenge.

Endive
PREPARING FOR GRILL

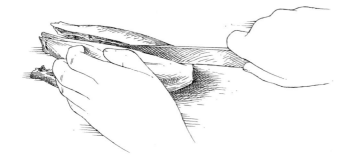

❶ With a knife, shave off the discolored end of the endive. Cut the thinnest slice possible.

❷ Cut the endive in half length-wise through the core end.

Extracts
ADDING TINY AMOUNTS

Tip 205

It is difficult to measure small amounts of extracts and food colorings. A baby medicine dropper lets you measure and disperse minute amounts evenly over a batter or icing.

Slowly squeeze the liquid from the medicine dropper into the bowl, letting drops fall in various spots on the surface of the batter.

Fennel
PREPARING

Tip 206

The bulb is the part of this odd-looking vegetable that is used in most recipes. Here's how to trim the stalks and remove the tough core from the bulb.

Cut off the stems and ❶ feathery fronds. (The fronds can be minced and used for garnishing.)

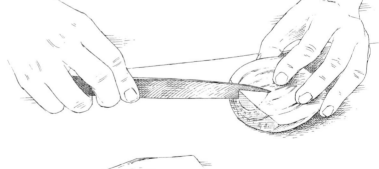

Trim a thin slice from the ❷ base of the bulb and remove any tough or blemished outer layers of the bulb. Cut the bulb in half through the base and use a paring knife to cut out the pyramid-shaped piece of the core in each half. The fennel bulb can now be sliced or chopped as desired.

Fennel Seeds
CHOPPING NEATLY

Tip 207

❶ Place the measured seeds in a small pile on a cutting board. Pour just enough water or oil on the seeds to moisten them.

Small, hard seeds like fennel and cumin are seemingly impossible to chop because they scatter all over the counter when you bear down on them. Here's how to overcome this problem.

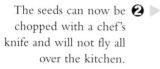

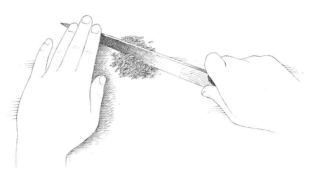

The seeds can now be **❷** chopped with a chef's knife and will not fly all over the kitchen.

Tip 208

Fish
SKINNING FILLETS

Removing the skin from fillets can be a tricky job. Here's how to make this task easier.

Starting at the thin end of the fillet, slide a knife between the skin and flesh until you can grab hold of the skin with a paper towel. Use this "handle" to help steady the skin as you continue to cut the flesh away from it.

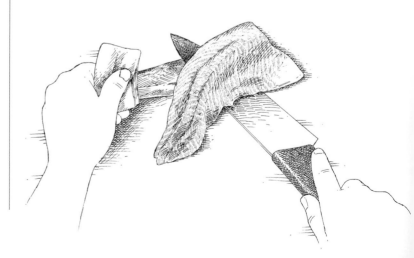

Fish
COOKING THIN FILLETS

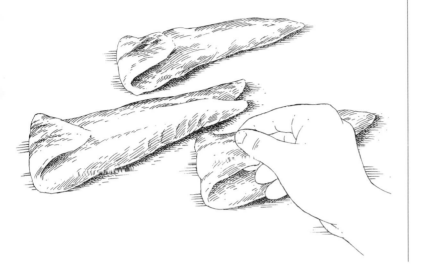

Many fillets taper down to a thin end, which is prone to overcooking. Here's an easy way to ensure even cooking throughout the fillet.

Fold the thin tail piece over so that the fillet is now an even thickness from end to end. Once the tail has been folded, place the fish in a hot skillet, folded-side up.

Fish
GRILLING WHOLE FISH

A whole grilled fish is apt to dry out if overcooked. But how do you check the flesh without tearing through the skin? We find that this method not only allows us to peek into the flesh but also promotes even cooking.

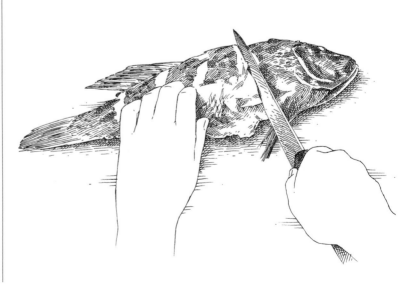

Once a fish is scaled and gutted, use a sharp knife to make shallow diagonal slashes every 2 inches along both sides of the fish from top to bottom, beginning just behind the dorsal fin.

Fish

EASY TRANSFER

Grilling a large fillet or a whole fish can prove a challenge when it comes to turning the fish or removing it from the grill without having it fall apart. Here are two solutions to this problem.

Tip 211

Once the fish is done, slide two metal spatulas under the belly to give it proper support, lifting gently to make sure the skin is not sticking to the grill. Quickly lift the fish and place it on a nearby platter.

Tip 212

❶ Before grilling, place the fish on a length of cheesecloth that is about 4 to 6 inches longer than the fish.

❷ Wrap the fish carefully, then tie the cheesecloth shut at both ends with string; grill as directed.

❸ Though the cheesecloth will turn brown, the overhang creates handles that extend over the edges of the grill, making turning or lifting the fish risk-free.

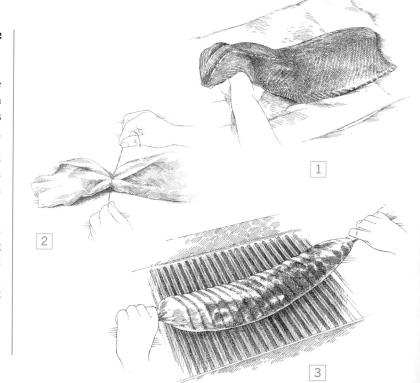

Tip 213

Filleting a whole cooked fish is not difficult. A few cuts with a sharp knife and a metal spatula do the trick.

Fish
FILLETING WHOLE FISH

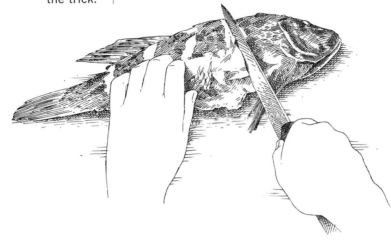

▲ **❶** Using a sharp knife, make a vertical cut just behind the head from the top of the fish to the belly. Make another cut along the top of the fish from the head to the tail.

▼ **❷** Use a metal spatula to lift the meat from the bones, starting at the head end and running the spatula over the bones to lift out the fillet. Repeat on the other side of the fish. Discard the fish head and skeleton.

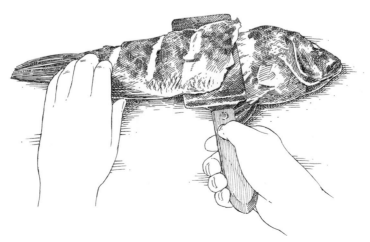

It's not difficult to cut a whole halibut steak into 4 boneless portions. Use the long bone running down the center of the fish as a guide.

Run a knife along the sides of the long bone running down the center of the fish, then follow the line of the thin membrane that crosses the bone, separating it from the flesh.

Fish *Halibut*
PREPARING BONED STEAKS

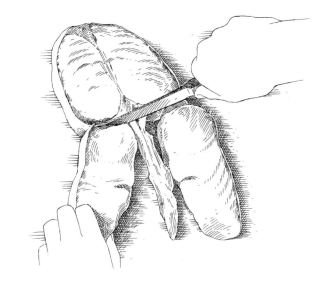

A flame tamer is a metal disk that can be used as a buffer between a burner and a pot to maintain a gentle, low level of heat. A flame tamer is especially useful when trying to cook a stew, soup, or sauce at the barest simmer for a long time. Aluminum foil can be fashioned into a thick, slightly flattened ring and placed right on top of a gas burner.

Flame Tamer
MAKING A FOIL RING

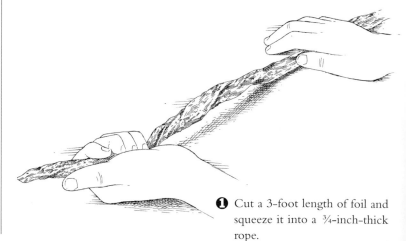

❶ Cut a 3-foot length of foil and squeeze it into a ¾-inch-thick rope.

Tip 216

This is how we store flours, as well as sugar, in our test kitchen. This tip speeds up the measuring process and keeps our counters clean.

Place flours in wide-mouth plastic containers with airtight lids. When you need to measure flour, simply dip the cup into the flour and then sweep the overflow back into the container.

Flour
STORING IN A WIDE-MOUTH CONTAINER

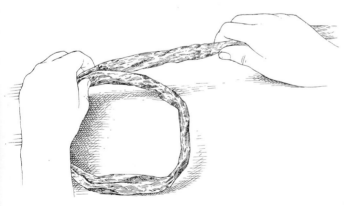

❷ Roll one end to form a ring the size of the burner.

❸ Twist the remaining foil rope around the ring to form a flame tamer. Set the ring on the burner, then place the pot on top.

Flour
SUMMER STORAGE

Those who live in humid climates probably know firsthand that flour absorbs moisture from the air, which in turn adds weight when you weigh it out for a recipe. Try these storage methods to ensure accurate weight measurements.

Tip 217

Store the flour in its bag in the freezer. This method also eliminates the possibility of bug infestation.

Tip 218

If you're short on freezer space, store the flour in your microwave oven. When you need to use the microwave, just remove the flour and replace it when you're finished.

Flour

STORING AND MEASURING BOXED FLOUR

Bakers who make cakes infrequently may not have a covered storage container, especially for cake flour. This storage idea not only keeps flour fresh, it makes measuring the flour a less messy chore.

Transfer the flour from the box to a large, heavy-duty zipper-lock bag. Seal the bag, then store it in the original box. When you need some flour, simply lift the bag out of the box and dip the measuring cup right in.

Flour

NO-FUSS FLOURING

Tip 220

Hauling out a large container can be a nuisance when all you have to do is dust a cake pan or work surface with some flour. Use this tip for confectioners' sugar as well.

Set a funnel in an empty glass salt shaker and scoop a little flour into the funnel. When the shaker has been filled, seal it and store it in the pantry. These small shakers are easy to reach and do an excellent job of lightly coating a surface with flour.

When sifting flour into a bowl, it's likely that some of the flour will end up making a dusty mess of your countertop. Here's a way to cut back on the mess.

Overturn your flour canister lid to use as a "coaster" for your sifter. When finished, simply empty the flour from the lid back into the canister.

Flour
SIFTER COASTER

Flour
ADDING FLOUR IN INCREMENTS

Many food processor bread recipes call for adding flour in small increments. It can be a real pain to unlock the lid and add flour several times.

Tip 222

Before adding any flour, we shape a doubled piece of parchment or waxed paper into a funnel and then slide it into the feed tube of the food processor. Flour can now be added as needed to the funnel, and it will flow slowly, evenly, and steadily into the workbowl.

Flour
COATING CUTTERS

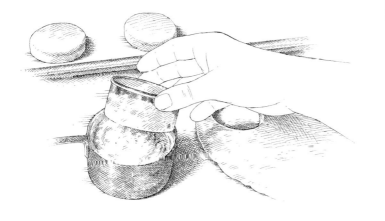

Recipes for biscuits and cookies often call for dipping the cutter in flour between cuttings. Here's how we do this in our test kitchen, without dirtying an extra bowl.

Fill the cup measure (which is already dirty from measuring flour for the cookies or biscuits) with more flour. As you work, simply dip the cutter into the measuring cup, which is the perfect shape and size.

Tip 224

Focaccia
DIMPLING THE DOUGH

Unlike pizza, focaccia is topped not by a sauce but with olive oil and herbs or other small pieces of topping. Without a sauce to anchor the toppings, they are likely to slip off the cooked focaccia. This method keeps the toppings in place.

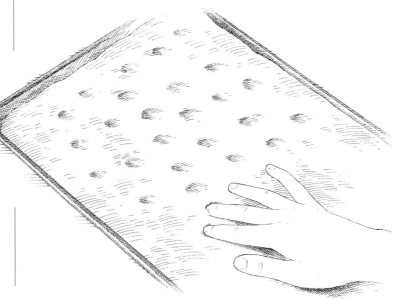

After the second rise, wet two fingers and use them to make indentations at regular intervals across the dough. The dimples should be deep enough to hold pieces of topping.

Food Processor
KEEPING THE LID CLEAN

Tip 225

Everyone knows that food processors save time in the kitchen, but cleaning them can be a real chore. Here's a neat way to keep the lid clean and thus eliminate washing time.

Place all ingredients in the ❶ workbowl and then cover the bowl with a sheet of plastic wrap.

Fit the lid onto the work- ❷ bowl, making sure that the plastic wrap lines the entire lid. Process as directed. When done, simply lift off the clean lid and discard the splattered sheet of plastic.

Food Processor
POURING LIQUIDS FROM THE WORKBOWL

Tip 226

Pouring liquids from the workbowl can be tricky. You don't want to remove the blade (and get your hands dirty), but if you don't the blade will fall out. Here's how to keep the blade safely in the workbowl as you pour.

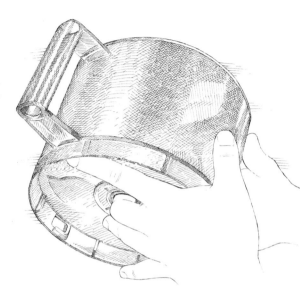

Remove the workbowl from **❶** the food processor when the liquid has been processed. Hold the bowl with one hand and push your finger into the bowl shaft and the hollow of the blade.

The bowl can now be turned **❷** upside down to pour out the contents while your finger keeps the blade in place.

Food Processor
CLEANING THE WORKBOWL

The easiest way to clean bowls is to soak them with water before washing. However, the hole in the center of a food processor workbowl makes this impossible to do. Here's a way to plug up that hole.

Remove the bowl cover ❶ 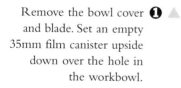 and blade. Set an empty 35mm film canister upside down over the hole in the workbowl.

Now you can fill the bowl ❷ ▷ with warm, soapy water and allow it to soak.

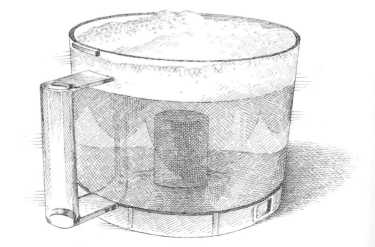

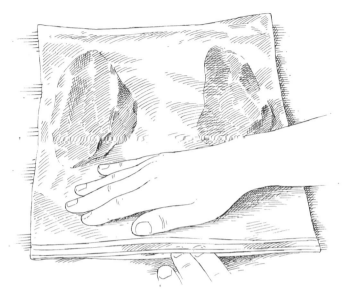

Freezer
FREEZING SMALLER PORTIONS

Tip 228

For cooks feeding small families, or perhaps just one person, freezing in small batches is a must. Here's a good way to freeze in small batches using large, freezer-safe plastic bags. Use this technique with chicken cutlets, steaks, or ground meats.

Place two portions of food in ❶ ▲ different locations inside a large zipper-lock freezer bag. Flatten the bag, forcing air out in the process, so that the portions do not touch.

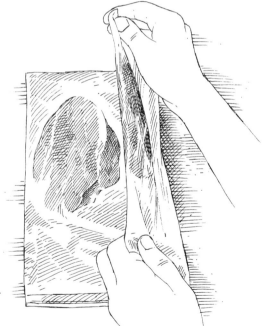

Fold the bag over in the ❷ ▶ center and freeze. The bag divides the two portions so they will freeze separately. Best of all, you have the choice of using one or both frozen portions.

Freezer
KEEPING TRACK OF FROZEN FOODS

Most cooks have put something in the freezer only to forget about it completely, then thrown away the freezer-burned mystery parcel months later. Here's an easy way to keep track of what's in your freezer.

Every time you put something in the freezer, add the name of the food and the date to a list clipped to the freezer door. The list is a constant reminder and will inspire you to use up those frozen goodies.

Freezer
FREEING UP CONTAINERS

Plastic food storage containers are at a premium in many kitchens. Unfortunately, many of these containers end up in the freezer for months. Here's how to liberate the containers from the freezer.

❶ Pass the container under hot running water just long enough to release its contents in a frozen block.

Drop the frozen block into a ❷ zipper-lock freezer bag, seal the bag, and return the food to the freezer.

Garbage Disposal
— Hors d'Oeuvres

Garbage Disposal
MAKESHIFT FUNNEL TRAP

Cooks who have a garbage disposal often peel and pare vegetables and fruits right over the sink. Of course, this likely means they have at some point also dropped the item they were paring into the disposal's wide drain hole. Take this precaution next time.

Position a small funnel in the drain hole. The funnel, with a diameter just slightly larger than that of the drain opening, catches the desirable pieces of food.

Garlic

NO-FUSS FLAVOR BOOST

Here's a no-fuss way to add the flavor of garlic to a soup, stew, or other such dish.

Rub the papery outer layer of skin off an intact head of garlic, cut about ½ inch off the top to expose the flesh of the cloves, and throw the whole head into the soup pot. When the soup is done, remove the garlic head and either discard it or squeeze the softened garlic into the soup to further flavor and thicken it.

Garlic
DRY-TOASTING

Here's a simple way to tame that harsh garlic flavor and also loosen the skins for easy peeling. For garlic with a creamier texture (akin to roasted garlic), increase the toasting time to 15 minutes.

❶ Place unpeeled garlic cloves in a dry skillet over medium–high heat. Toast, shaking the pan occasionally, until the skins are golden brown, about 5 minutes. Transfer the toasted cloves to a cutting board and cool.

❷ When cooled, the once-clingy skins peel off readily. The garlic can now be sliced, chopped, or minced and used as you normally would, but it will have far less bite.

SAFE PEELING

One effective method for peeling garlic is to crush the cloves
using the broad side of a knife blade. While this method is perfectly safe if
you treat the knife blade with care, some may prefer skipping the knife altogether.

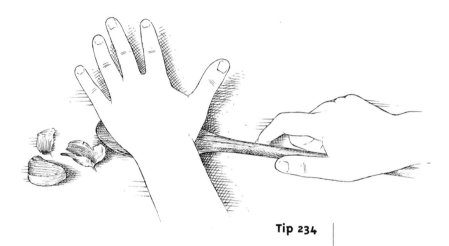

Tip 234

Cover the garlic clove with the concave side of a wooden
spoon and press down hard. The cup of the spoon prevents the
garlic clove from shooting out across the work surface.

Tip 235

Alternatively, whack the clove
with the bottom of a can.
The weight of the contents
helps crush the clove, and the
lip at the bottom of the can
keeps the clove neatly in
place on the work surface.

Garlic
EASY PEELING

Tip 236

An old-fashioned rubber jar opener can be used instead of a cannoli-style rubber garlic peeler.

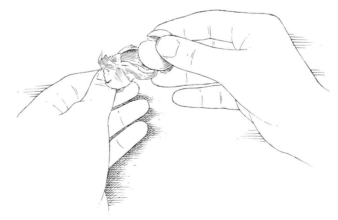

▲ **❶** Place one or two cloves in the center of the jar opener.

◀ **❷** Roll the cloves around inside the soft, thin rubber.

▼ **❸** The friction created by the rubber will cause the paper-like skin of the garlic to slip right off.

Garlic
CLEANING A PRESS

Dirty garlic presses are notoriously challenging to clean. Here's an easy way to accomplish this task and recycle an old toothbrush.

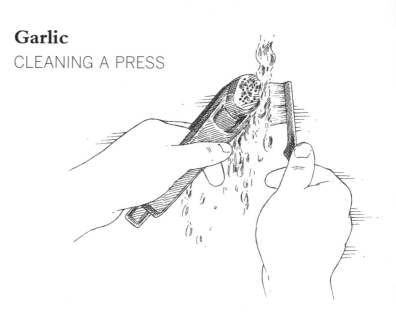

Once the bristles are worn, clean the toothbrush well and keep it in a handy spot in the kitchen to clean bits of garlic from a press. A toothbrush can also be used to clean tight or hard-to-reach spots in other kitchen utensils.

Garlic
MAKING A SMALL AMOUNT OF PUREE

If you just need a dab of pureed garlic for a vinaigrette, try this handy technique.

❶ Hold a fork with its tines resting face-down just above a cutting board. Rub a peeled clove of garlic rapidly back and forth against the tines, close to their points.

Once the clove has been **❷** broken down, turn the fork over and mash any large chunks to make a smooth puree.

Here's how to produce very fine, smooth bits of garlic without a garlic press. If possible, use kosher or coarse salt; the larger crystals do a better job of breaking down the garlic than fine table salt.

Garlic
MINCING TO A PASTE

❶ Mince the garlic as you normally would on a cutting board. Sprinkle the minced garlic with salt.

❷ Drag the side of a chef's knife over the garlic salt mixture to form a fine puree. Continue to mince and drag the knife as necessary until the puree is smooth.

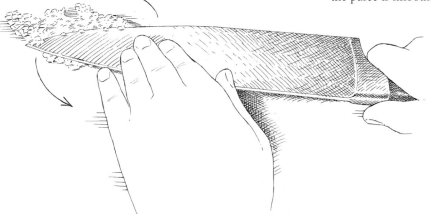

Ginger
PEELING

Because of its shape, ginger can be difficult to peel, especially if using a knife. Try this method to reduce waste.

Use the bowl of a teaspoon to scrape off the knotty skin from a knob of ginger. The spoon moves easily around curves in the ginger, so you remove just the skin.

Tip 241

To produce large amounts of ginger juice for dressings or sauces, you must wrap grated ginger in cheesecloth and squeeze. If you need just a teaspoon or two of ginger juice, try this method.

Ginger
JUICING

Cut off a small piece of ❶ peeled ginger from a large knob. Place the piece, about the size of a large garlic clove, into a garlic press.

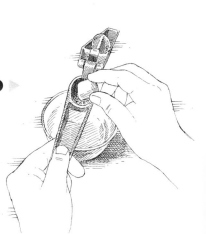

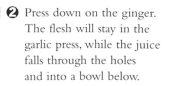

❷ Press down on the ginger. The flesh will stay in the garlic press, while the juice falls through the holes and into a bowl below.

Ginger
MINCING

Ginger is highly fibrous, which makes it tricky to mince. A sharp knife is a must. This technique works best.

❶ Slice the peeled knob of ginger into thin rounds, then fan the rounds out and cut them into thin matchstick-like strips.

❷ Chop the matchsticks crosswise into a fine mince.

Ginger
GRATING

Most cooks who use fresh ginger have scraped their fingers on the grater when the piece of ginger gets down to a tiny nub. Instead of cutting a small chunk of ginger off a larger piece and then grating it, try this method.

Peel a small section of the large piece of ginger. Grate the peeled portion, using the rest of the ginger as a handle to keep fingers safely away from the grater.

Ginger
SMASHING GINGER

Smashing ginger is a quick way to release its flavorful oils. This method works equally well with scallions that have been halved lengthwise.

Thinly slice an unpeeled knob and then use the end of a chef's knife to smash each piece.

Gnocchi
MAKING RIDGES

Tip 245

When making gnocchi, it's customary to give each piece distinct ridges using a butter paddle or the tines of a fork. This kitchen utensil works just as well.

Line up the gnocchi pieces on a work surface, then roll a whisk over them to create deep, even ridges.

Goose

RENDERING THE FAT

A goose has a thick layer of fat right under the skin that must be rendered in the oven. If the fat remains, the skin will be flabby and the meat greasy. This technique can be used with duck, too.

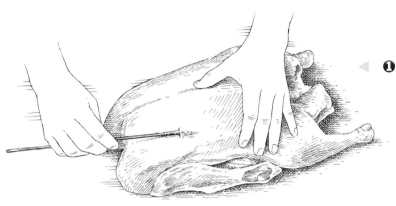

❶ With a trussing needle or skewer, prick the goose skin all over, especially around the breast and thighs. Hold the needle nearly parallel to the bird to avoid pricking the meat. These holes provide an exit route for rendered fat.

Using rubber gloves to protect **❷** your hands from possible splashes of boiling water, lower the goose, neck-end down, into a stockpot filled with simmering water, submerging as much of the goose as possible until "goose bumps" appear, about 1 minute. Repeat this process, submerging the goose tail-end down. Dry the goose with paper towels, then set it on a rack in a roasting pan and refrigerate for 1 to 2 days. The boiling and drying process tightens the skin so that during roasting the fat is squeezed out.

Greens
SEPARATING LEAVES FROM STEMS

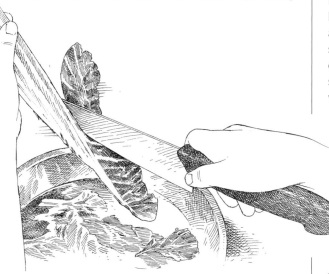

Leafy greens such as kale, mustard greens, and collards, have thick stems that must be discarded. Swiss chard stems do become tender when cooked. Here's a simple way to slice away the leaves from the thick central stalks.

Hold each leaf at the base of the stem over a bowl filled with water, and use a sharp knife to slash the leafy portion from either side of the thick stem.

Greens
SPACE SAVER FOR DRAINING

Many recipes for large-leaved greens such as kale and collards recommend adding the greens to the cooking pot with a little water from their washing still clinging to their leaves. Finding a place to temporarily store the bulky, wet leaves without turning your work surface into a watery mess can be a challenge.

As you wash the greens, remove them to the empty dish rack next to the sink.

Greens
DRYING BLANCHED GREENS

Many leafy greens, such as broccoli rabe and kale, benefit from quick submerging in boiling water (a process called blanching) before being sautéed with flavorings. After blanching, it's important to squeeze as much water as possible out of the greens before adding them to the pan. Instead of squeezing the greens by hand, try this method.

Place the wet greens in the **❶** ▲ hopper of a potato ricer.

Close the handle and **❷** ▶ squeeze the water from the greens. Don't squeeze harder than is necessary, or you might puree the greens.

Grilling
CHECKING THE FUEL LEVEL

There's nothing worse than running out of fuel halfway through grilling. If your grill doesn't have a gas gauge, use this technique to estimate how much gas is left in the tank.

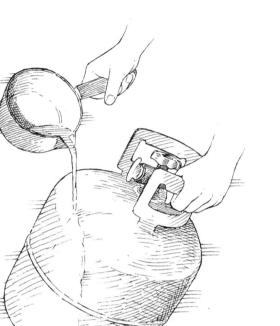

❶ Bring a cup or so of water to a boil in a small saucepan or glass measuring cup (if using the microwave). Pour the water over the side of the tank.

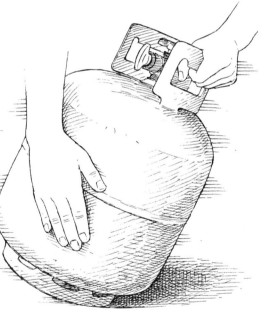

❷ Feel the metal with your hand. Where the water has succeeded in warming the tank, it is empty; where the tank remains cool to the touch, there is still propane inside.

Grilling
LIGHTING THE FIRE

Our favorite tool for lighting a charcoal fire is called a chimney, or flue, starter. A chimney starter is shaped like a can, with both ends open. A wood handle on the side helps you move the can around the grill. Inside, a metal plate divides the lower portion (used to hold crumpled newspaper) from the upper portion (where the charcoal rests).

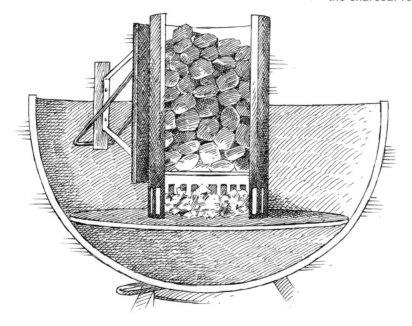

To use a chimney starter, place two or three crumpled sheets of newspaper in the bottom section. Set the starter on the bottom grate in a kettle grill and fill the main compartment with as much charcoal as directed in individual recipes. When you light the newspaper, the flames will shoot up through the charcoal and ignite it. When the coals are covered with light gray ash, they are ready. Simply dump the coals onto the grate and arrange as necessary, using long-handled tongs.

Grilling
EASY PREPARATION

Hoisting a huge bag of charcoal to pour some into a chimney starter can be messy and difficult, especially when you are dressed nicely for a summer dinner party. Some advance preparation streamlines the process.

When you bring home the sack from the ❶ ▲ store, divide the briquettes into smaller bags, about 4 quarts (50 briquettes) to a bag.

When you need to build a fire, just cut a large ❷ ▼ hole in the bottom of a smaller bag. The charcoal flows right into the chimney, without making a mess or straining your back.

Grilling
RESTARTING A FIRE

When your charcoal fire peters out before really getting started, you can douse the coals with lighter fluid, toss in a match, and create a thrilling fireball, or you can try this safer, tamer method.

Turn an electric hair dryer to high and aim it toward the base of the pile of coals. The air flow acts as a bellows to get the fire going again in just a few minutes.

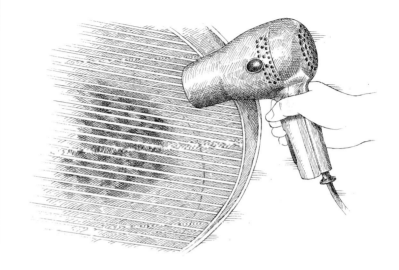

Grilling
MEASURING CHARCOAL FOR GRILLING

Many recipes call for a particular volume of charcoal, such as 4 quarts. Here's an easy way to measure it out.

Open the top of an empty half-gallon carton of milk or juice and wash the carton thoroughly. Store this carton with the charcoal and use it as a measure. Each full carton equals roughly 2 quarts.

Grilling
MAKING YOUR OWN CHIMNEY STARTER

Although a chimney starter is relatively inexpensive, you may want to save money and improvise with an empty 39-ounce coffee can that has had both ends removed with a can opener. Note that there are two drawbacks to this method. The improvised starter has no handles so you must maneuver it with long-handled tongs. Also, because of its size, this improvised starter can't light enough charcoal for most grilling jobs; you will need to add unlit coals once the lit coals have been dumped onto the charcoal grate.

Grilling
LIGHTING A FIRE WITHOUT A CHIMNEY STARTER

Our preferred method for lighting charcoal calls for a chimney starter. If you don't have a starter, try this.

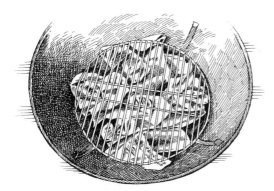

❶ Place 8 crumpled sheets of newspaper beneath the grate on which the charcoal sits.

❷ With the bottom air vents open, pile the charcoal on the grate, then light the paper. After about 20 minutes, the coals should be covered with light gray ash and ready for cooking.

❶ Using a church-key can opener, punch six holes along the lower circumference of the can.

❷ Set the can on the grill's charcoal rack with the triangular holes at the bottom. Load the can about one-half to two-thirds full with crumpled newspaper, then top it off with charcoal.

❸ Insert a long match through one of the triangular holes at the bottom to set the crumpled paper on fire.

❹ When the coals are lit (after about 20 minutes), use tongs to grasp the top of the starter and dump its contents onto the charcoal rack. Place more coals loosely around and on top of the burning coals to build up a cooking fire.

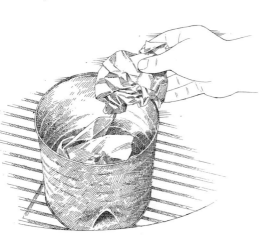

Grilling
BUILDING A TWO-LEVEL FIRE

In many cases, we like to grill over a two-level fire. With this arrangement, one part of the grill is very hot, while the other side is cooler. This setup works well for chops and chicken parts, which can be seared on the hot part of the grill and then cooked through more slowly on the cool part without causing the exterior to char. Having a cool section of the grill also gives the cook a place to drag foods if flames engulf the hot section.

To build a two-level fire, pile the lit charcoal on half of the grill and leave the other half free of coals. Use long-handled tongs to move briquettes into place as necessary.

Grilling
MAKING A PACKET FOR WOOD CHIPS

Hickory, mesquite, and other wood chips can be added to a charcoal fire to flavor foods. Here's the best way to keep the chips burning slowly and thus prolong their smoking time.

❶ Soak the chips in a bowl of water for at least 1 hour to slow down the rate at which they will burn. Drain the chips and place them in the center of an 18-inch square of aluminum foil. Fold in all four sides of the foil to completely enclose the chips.

❷ Turn the foil packet over. Tear about six large holes (each the size of a quarter) through the top of the foil packet with a fork to allow smoke to escape. Place the packet, with the holes facing up, directly on top of a pile of lit charcoal.

Food that is being grilled is much less likely to stick to a clean grate. We recommend cleaning the hot grate with a wire brush designed specifically for that purpose, but if you find yourself without a brush, this method also gets the job done.

A pair of tongs and a crumpled wad of aluminum foil will clean your grill grate beautifully.

Grilling
BRUSHLESS GRATE CLEANING

Grilling
OILING THE COOKING GRATE

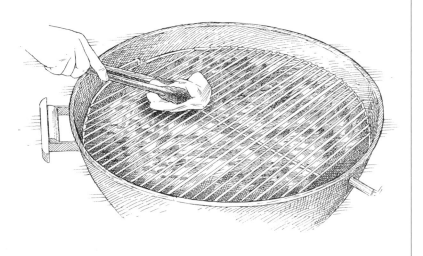

Once coals have been lit and spread out in the bottom of the grill, put the cooking grate in place, and let it heat up for several minutes. For foods such as fish, which tend to stick to the grill, take this extra precaution.

Dip a large wad of paper towels in vegetable oil, grab the wad with tongs, and wipe the grid thoroughly to lubricate it. This extra step also removes any remaining residue on the grate, which might mar the delicate flavor of fish.

Tip 261

Before grilling, use this technique to determine how hot your fire is. Some foods require a blazing hot fire, while others are best cooked over cooler coals.

Hold your hand 5 inches above the cooking grate. When the fire is hot, you won't be able to leave your hand there for more than 2 seconds; when the fire is medium, 4 or 5 seconds; and when the fire is medium-low, you will be able to leave your hand in place for about 7 seconds.

Grilling
MEASURING THE HEAT LEVEL

Tip 262

When grill-roasting a chicken or barbecuing ribs with the lid on, use this method to gauge the grill temperature. For poultry and small roasts, the temperature should be between 300 and 400 degrees. If slow-cooking ribs or thick roasts, keep the temperature between 200 and 300 degrees.

Put the food on the grill and set the lid in place. Open the air vents slightly and insert a grill thermometer through the vent.

Grilling
MEASURING THE HEAT IN A CLOSED KETTLE

Grilling
DOUSING FLAMES WITH A SQUIRT BOTTLE

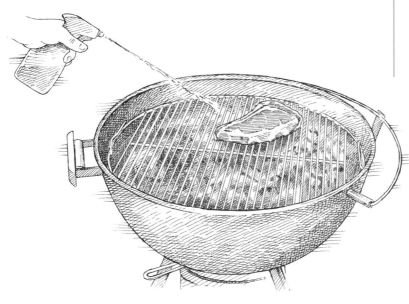

No one wants an uncontrolled fire that chars food on the grill. Here's an excellent way to prevent a grease fire from ruining your meal.

Keep a squirt bottle or plant mister filled with water near the grill. At the first sign of flames, try to pull foods to a cool part of the grill and douse the flames with water.

Tips 264 & 265

Not many households stock extra pastry brushes designated for basting, especially for foods on the grill. Here are two good substitutions.

Grilling
BASTING BRUSH IMPROVISATIONS

Tip 264

Try using a large lettuce leaf as a brush for marinades and sauces.

Grilling
SOAKING BAMBOO SKEWERS

Tip 266

Soaking bamboo skewers before grilling helps keep the wood from burning before the food is cooked. But when the skewers are placed in water, they tend to float to the surface. Here's how to keep them submerged.

Fill a rinsed-out 2-liter soda bottle with fresh water. Slip the skewers in the bottle and screw the cap in place. The skewers will remain submerged until you remove the cap.

Tip 265

Spear a juiced lemon half onto a fork. The lemon baster works especially well when you're basting with a lemony sauce.

Grilling
ONE PLATTER FOR TWO JOBS

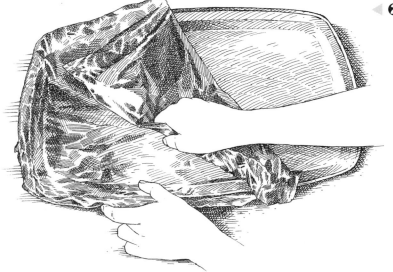

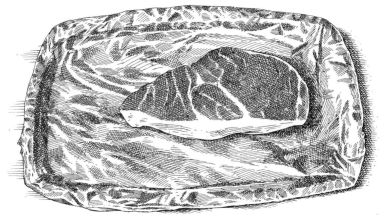

Tip 267

Grilled meat, poultry, and fish should not be returned to the same platter that was used to carry the raw food to the grill. Instead of last-minute fumbling for a new platter, this method uses a single platter for both jobs, which also saves on cleanup time.

❶ Cover the platter with foil before placing the raw food on it.

❷ While the food is grilling, remove the foil so you can use the same platter when the food comes off the grill.

Grilling
EASY ASH REMOVAL

No matter how you do it, emptying a kettle grill of cool ashes is a messy procedure. A homemade ash scoop can neaten up things.

❶ Cut off a bottom corner of a plastic milk jug to form a scoop.

❷ The plastic conforms to the curve of the grill bottom, which makes it easy to collect ashes with a single sweep.

Grilling
PROTECTING GAS CONTROLS

The ignition and burner control knobs on some gas grills can be persnickety if they get wet or dirty from exposure to the elements, especially if the grill is kept outdoors in the snow during the winter. If your grill has no cover, try this impromptu solution.

Invert a disposable aluminum roasting pan over the control panel and tape it in place on either end with duct or electrical tape.

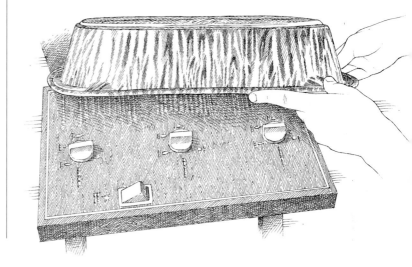

Guacamole
EASY AVOCADO MASHING

Instead of painstakingly mashing avocadoes with a fork when whipping up your next batch of guacamole, turn to this other convenient, low-tech kitchen tool.

A pastry blender mashes avocadoes quickly and the clean-up is just as quick.

Ham

HANDLING A COUNTRY HAM

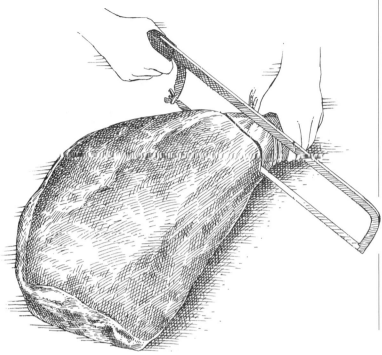

Tip 271

We love country ham but find its large size makes it unwieldy to cook, especially because the ham should be simmered in a stockpot before being roasted.

To get around this problem, use a hacksaw to remove the hock end of the ham. The ham should then fit into a large stockpot or roasting pan. Save the hock for cooking beans or greens or making soup.

Tip 272

After working with pungent ingredients such as garlic, onions, or fish, lemon juice helps to wash away any lingering odors from hands. When the odor is too strong for citrus, try this method.

Handwashing

DEODORIZER

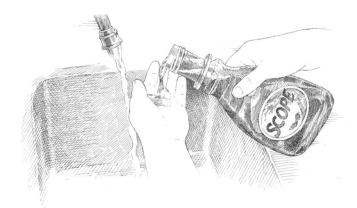

Wash your hands with a couple of tablespoons of mouthwash. Any inexpensive brand will do the job.

Hash Browns
FLIPPING SAFELY

Tip 273

Hash browns as well as Chinese noodle cakes and Spanish omelets must be browned on both sides in a hot skillet. Most recipes suggest inverting the food onto a plate and then sliding it back into the skillet to cook the second side. We find that the removable bottom of a metal tart pan works better than a plate.

Using an oven mitt or **❶** potholders, slide the tart pan bottom over the skillet and invert the skillet.

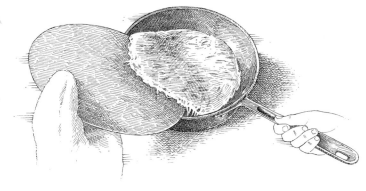

The tart pan bottom is easy **❷** to handle, lightweight, and has no rim or curvature, so the food slides back into the skillet easily.

Tip 274

Hazelnuts
TOASTING AND SKINNING

Hazelnuts are covered with a dark brown skin that can be quite bitter. Toasting the nuts in a 350-degree oven until fragrant (about 15 minutes) improves their flavor and also causes the skins to blister and crack so they can be rubbed off.

Transfer the toasted nuts to ❶ ▲
the center of a clean tea towel.

Bring up the sides of the towel and twist it ❷ ▶
closed to seal in the nuts.

Rub the nuts together in the towel to scrape ❸ ▶
off as much of the brown skin as possible to
reveal the light-colored nutmeats. It's fine if
patches of skin remain.

Carefully open the towel on ❹ ▼
a flat surface. Gently roll the
nuts away from the skins.

Herbs
ADDING FLAVOR

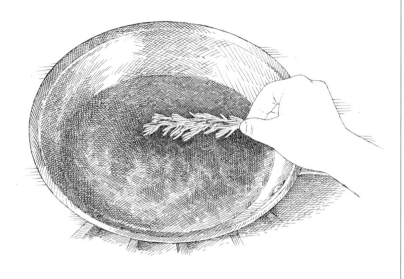

Tip 275

Here's a no-fuss way to add the flavor of hardy herbs to a soup, stew, chowder, or sauce.

In recipes that call for thyme or rosemary, there's no need to strip the leaves off the branches and mince them. Simply throw the whole branch into the pan. Remember to remove the spent branch, as you would spent bay leaves, before serving. Rosemary is very strong, so you may want to keep it in the pot for only 15 minutes or so.

Herbs
RELEASING FLAVOR FROM DRIED HERBS

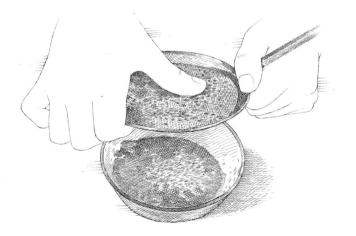

Tip 276

Flavorful oils in dried oregano, thyme, and other herbs should be released before the herbs are added to foods. You can crush dried herbs between your fingers or use this method for maximum flavor.

Place the dried herbs in a mesh sieve and push down on them with your fingertips as you shake the sieve back and forth over a bowl.

A bouquet garni is a classic French combination of herbs and spices used to flavor soups, stocks, and stews. Traditional recipes call for wrapping the herbs and spices in cheesecloth for easy removal before serving. A coffee filter, which most modern cooks are more likely to have on hand, can be used in place of the cheesecloth.

Herbs

MAKING A BOUQUET GARNI

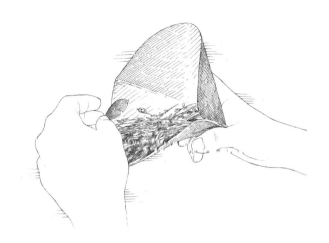

❶ Place the herbs (usually bay leaves and thyme, either dried or fresh, and fresh parsley) and spices (usually black peppercorns) into the coffee filter.

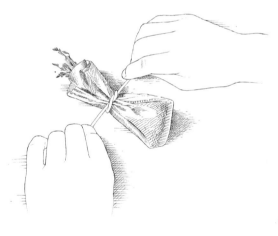

❷ Tie the end of the coffee filter closed, catching the stems of the herbs as you do so.

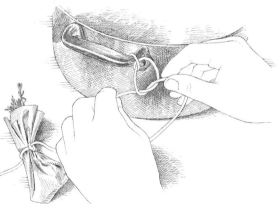

❸ Tie the other end of the string to the handle of the pot or pan so you can easily retrieve the bouquet garni once the herbs and spices have given up their flavor.

Herbs
HANDY SCISSORS FOR GARDEN CLIPPING

If you're tired of trekking back into the house for the scissors you forgot to bring into the garden, try this handy solution.

Bend a wire coat hanger or heavy floral wire to form a stand with a hooked end. Stick the wire in the soil and hang a small pair of inexpensive scissors on it and they'll be there whenever you are.

Herbs
STORING HARDY HERBS

Perennials such as sage
and thyme are hardy
enough to tolerate cold
outdoor temperatures,
and thus can be stored
in the refrigerator.

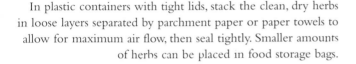

In plastic containers with tight lids, stack the clean, dry herbs
in loose layers separated by parchment paper or paper towels to
allow for maximum air flow, then seal tightly. Smaller amounts
of herbs can be placed in food storage bags.

Herbs
STORING DELICATE
HERBS

Tip 280

Delicate leafy herbs
like basil, cilantro, mint,
and the like should be
stored in water in the
refrigerator, but not in a
drinking glass. This set-up
will be top-heavy and
prone to slips and spills.

For a more stable herb
container, cut off the
top of a plastic 1-quart
or ½-gallon milk or
water jug.

Herbs
ALTERNATE USES FOR FRESH HERBS

Fresh herbs such as parsley or basil are sold in bunches much larger than needed to make just one or two recipes. Cut down on rotting herbs in your refrigerator with this idea.

In place of lettuce or other greens, use fresh herbs to give your sandwich an unexpected flavor boost.

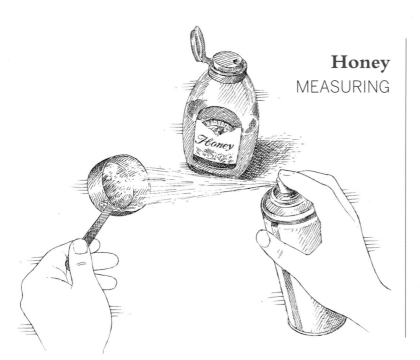

Honey
MEASURING

Sticky ingredients like honey and molasses take their time flowing out of a measuring cup and require a spoon to scrape out the remaining bits. This method makes neat and quick work of the task.

Spray the measuring cup with nonstick cooking spray before filling it. When emptied, the liquid will slip right out of the cup.

Hors d'Oeuvres
EDIBLE TOOTHPICKS

Any number of hors d'oeuvres—including small meatballs, crab cakes, marinated mushrooms, and bits of semisoft cheese—are served with toothpick skewers. We like this innovative alternative that avoids the problem of used toothpick disposal.

In place of wooden toothpicks, spear your hors d'oeuvres with slender pretzel sticks, which can be eaten right along with the tasty tidbit it has just skewered.

Hors d'Oeuvres
SAUCE BOWL STABILIZER

Many hors d'oeuvres—from crudites to shrimp cocktail to chips and salsa—involve small bowls of dipping sauce that can slide all over the platter, disrupting the carefully arranged tidbits (especially if the platter is being transported to a different location.)
    Add some stability to your next platter.

❶ Dab a bit of creamed honey on the bottom of the bowl you'll use to hold the dipping sauce.

❷ Secure the bowl to the platter, and arrange the food for dipping around it.

Ice Cream — Knives

Ice Cream

LEAK-FREE CONES

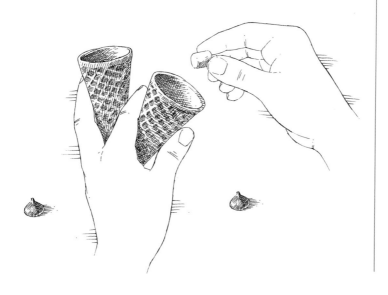

Children and adults who savor ice cream cones slowly know that the melting ice cream often saturates the tip of the cone, which can result in a messy leak. Here's how to keep the cone dry.

Place a mini marshmallow or upside-down Hershey's Kiss in each cone before loading it up with ice cream, creating a barrier between the melting ice cream and the fragile cone tip.

Ice Cream

KEEPING FRESH

If not eaten right way, ice cream can lose its fresh taste and form ice crystals on the surface as it sits in the freezer. An extra layer of insulation prevents this from happening.

Before returning the ice cream to the freezer, cover the portion remaining in the carton with heavy-duty plastic wrap, pressing the wrap flush against the surface of the ice cream. Replace the carton cover and return it to the freezer.

Ice Cream
QUICK AND EASY SINGLE SCOOPS

Some home refrigerators freeze ice cream so hard that the ice cream has to sit on the counter to soften before it can be scooped. To avoid the wait, we like this advance preparation method.

❶ Scoop fresh ice cream into a muffin tin lined with muffin papers, and then freeze.

Once frozen, the paper-lined **❷** portions can be stored in a plastic bag in the freezer for easy, ready-when-you-are servings. Just peel off the paper and place the ice cream in a bowl. This is also a great method for quickly firming up homemade ice cream, which is notoriously soft when it comes out of the machine.

Ice Cream
SERVING SUGGESTION

Tip 288

Taken straight from the freezer, small pint-sized containers of premium ice cream often are frozen too hard to scoop easily. Next time you're faced with this problem, try this creative solution.

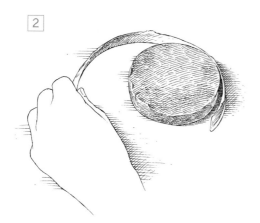

❶ Place the ice cream container on its side on a cutting board and cut off slices, right through the cardboard, with a serrated or electric knife.

❷ Peel the cardboard off the sides of the ice cream disk and serve. The lid will sit flush up against the ice cream left in the container for easy storage.

❸ The slice-and-serve method also lends itself to artful presentation. Cut the disks into interesting shapes using cookie cutters.

Tip 289

A simple glaze of milk or lemon juice mixed with powdered sugar adds a flavorful finish to quick breads, muffins, cinnamon buns, and the like, but mixing and applying the glaze can be a messy process. We like this neater method, which also eliminates the need to dirty a bowl and utensil.

Icing
MESS-FREE GLAZING

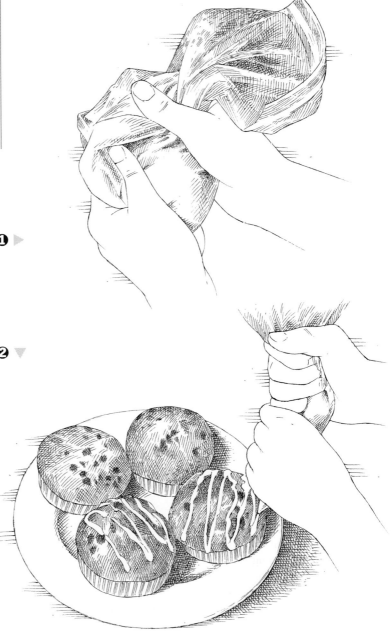

Add the powdered sugar and **❶** ▷
liquid to a zipper-lock sandwich bag, seal it, and knead the ingredients into a soft glaze.

To apply the glaze with **❷** ▽
precision, just snip off a small corner of the bag and squeeze.

Instant-Read Thermometer
RECALIBRATING

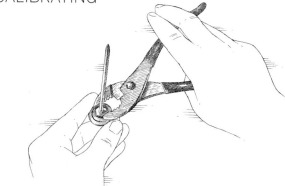

There's no point in using an instant-read thermometer if it's not accurate. To test accuracy, insert the probe into a pan of boiling water. The thermometer should register 212 degrees at sea level. (The boiling point drops about one degree for every 500-foot increase in altitude, so compensate accordingly.) If your dial-face thermometer is inaccurate, it can be adjusted.

Turn over the thermometer and use a pair of pliers to adjust the nut beneath the head. Keep adjusting until the thermometer reads 212 degrees when inserted into boiling water.

Instant-Read Thermometer
PROTECTING HANDS FROM POTS

Most instant-read thermometers come in a protective plastic sleeve with a metal clip (for clipping to aprons) that forms a loop at the very top. Use this clip and plastic sleeve to distance your hand from hot pots when taking a temperature.

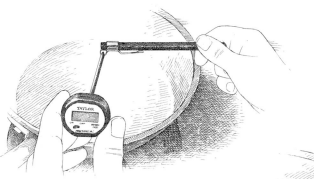

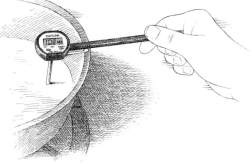

❶ Slide the probe end of the thermometer into the loop at the tip of the clip.

❷ Hold the end of the plastic sleeve to keep the thermometer upright, and then lower the probe into the food.

Instant-Read Thermometer
MEASURING SHALLOW LIQUIDS

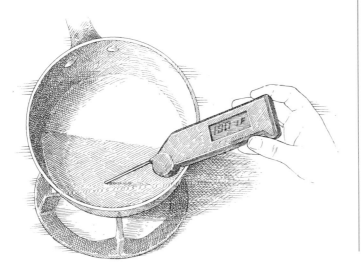

Recipes for custards, curds, pastry creams, and other delicate or heat-sensitive mixtures often indicate the temperature at which the mixture should be taken off the heat. If you are cooking a small quantity, use this technique to get an accurate reading with an instant-read thermometer.

Tilt the pan so that the liquid collects on one side, creating enough depth to get an accurate reading.

When making jams and jellies from fruits such as grapes, cherries, and plums, it's necessary to juice some of the fruit, but it can be difficult to do without nicking the seeds or pits, which, when cut, release bitter flavors into the fruit. Try this gentler method.

Fit a food processor with the short plastic dough blade. The processor will break down the fruit without nicking the seeds or pits.

Jam
JUICING FRUIT FOR JAM

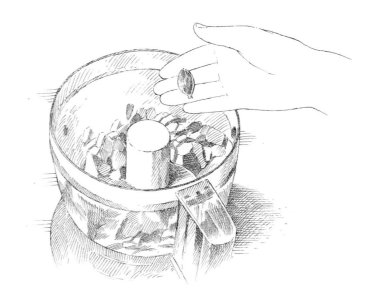

Jell-O
UNMOLDING SALADS

Jell-O salads can be difficult to remove from their molds. Using a mold with a hollow center, such as a Bundt pan, will make things easier, as will following these steps.

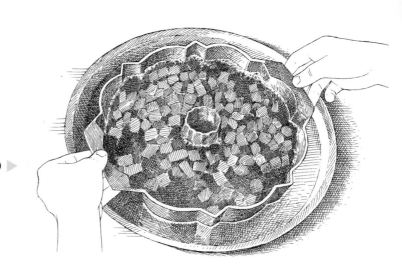

Gently lower the bottom of ❶ ▷ the mold into a bowl filled with hot water and keep it in place for about 5 seconds.

◁ ❷ With your finger, lightly press the edges of the Jell-O away from the mold to loosen the salad from the pan.

Place a large serving plate on ❸ ▷ top of the mold. Holding the plate securely in place, carefully invert the mold and release the Jell-O salad onto the plate.

Tip 295

Jícama, often available in supermarkets, is a sweet, nutty root vegetable common in Mexican and South American cuisines. Jícama can be eaten raw or cooked and should be peeled just before using.

Jícama
PREPARING

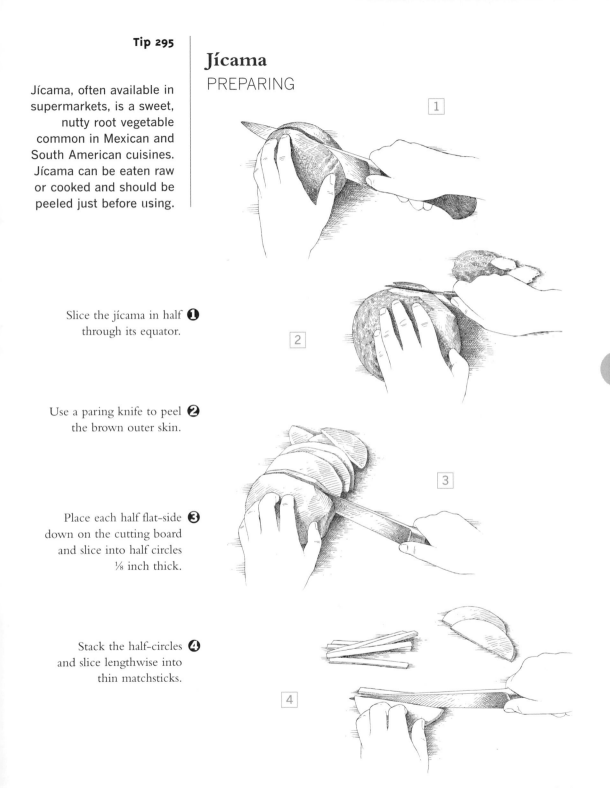

Slice the jícama in half ❶ through its equator.

Use a paring knife to peel ❷ the brown outer skin.

Place each half flat-side ❸ down on the cutting board and slice into half circles ⅛ inch thick.

Stack the half-circles ❹ and slice lengthwise into thin matchsticks.

Kitchen Efficiency
PROTECTING SINKS FROM CRACKS AND CHIPS

With soapy, slippery hands, it's easy to drop a heavy pot or pan into the sink while you're washing it. If you have a porcelain or enameled sink, this can result in an ugly chip or crack.

To protect your sink, lay several wooden spoons in it to cushion the blow in case you drop a heavy pot or pan.

Kitchen Efficiency
HOMEMADE TIERED SHELF

Small items, such as spice jars or extract bottles, can get lost in a well-stocked cabinet. Here's how to keep all items, even those at the back, visible at a glance.

Stack 2-by-4 pieces of lumber, cut to the right length, to create different height levels within the cabinet. Stack more wood in the back of the cabinet so that items in the rear will be visible above those placed in the front.

Kitchen Efficiency
SECURING THE SILVERWARE TRAY

Tip 298

Most silverware organizers are shorter than the drawers they're meant to organize. The result is that the organizer and its contents slide to the back of the drawer every time you open it. If you are tired of pulling the organizer forward all the time, here's how to anchor it to the drawer.

◀ **1** Affix several small pieces of poster tack, putty, or florist's clay (available at craft stores or flower shops) to the bottom of the organizer.

▼ **2** Press the tray into place in the drawer and fill as usual. The organizer will stay put, with no more sliding when you open and shut the drawer.

Kitchen Efficiency
STORING BOXES OF FOIL AND WRAP

The boxes containing plastic sandwich bags, rolls of tin foil, plastic wrap, and the like can use up a lot of valuable drawer space. Here's an efficient way to store these boxes in a cabinet under the counter.

Store the boxes upright in the slots of a cardboard six-pack container that once held beer or soda bottles.

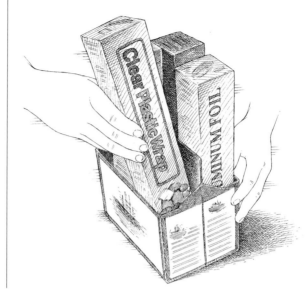

Kitchen Efficiency
SPACE-SAVING STORAGE

Cooks with limited storage space will appreciate this method of storing baking sheets upright.

A metal vertical file holder is ideal for storing cutting boards and baking sheets. They not only take up less space but are easy to grab when you need one.

Kitchen Efficiency
PLASTIC PRODUCE BAG STORAGE

Tip 301

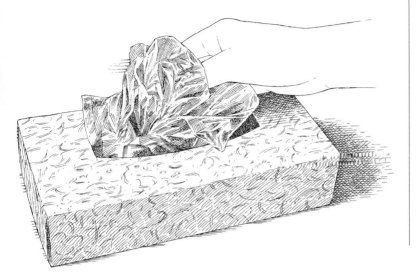

Many home kitchens sport a drawer filled to the gills with crumpled plastic produce bags. Reclaim your drawer with this space-saving solution.

Stuff the plastic bags into empty tissue boxes. A box will accommodate many, many bags, which are then easy to remove one at a time when the need arises.

Tip 302

Kitchen Efficiency
INSTANT COUNTER SPACE

No matter the size of the kitchen, a little extra counter space for resting bowls, platters, or cooling racks is always welcome.

Create extra counter space by opening a drawer and resting a cutting board across the top.

Kitchen Efficiency
ALTERNATIVE MISE EN PLACE CUPS

Cooking almost any recipe goes much faster when the ingredients are prepped, measured, and ready. The downside of laying out the ingredients, called *mise en place,* is that it means washing more dishes—bowls, ramekins, plates, and other containers. Here are some easy substitutes you can use for small quantities of ingredients.

Tip 303

Use flat-bottomed paper coffee filters in place of bowls or ramekins. When you are done, just throw the dirty filters in the trash. Paper cups can serve the same purpose.

Tip 304

If you are looking for a reusable alternative to ramekins, try clean, dry single-serving yogurt cups.

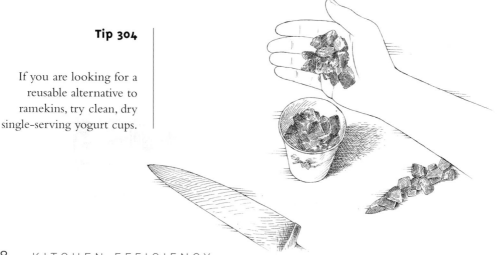

Kitchen Efficiency
SPACE-SAVING VEGETABLE PREP

Tip 305

If your kitchen is tight on counter space, it can be a hassle to prepare dishes like soups, stews, and stir-fries, all of which require a number of chopped vegetables and other ingredients.

Layer the chopped ingredients in a bowl in order of use, separating each layer with a sheet of wax paper or plastic wrap.

Tip 306

Kitchen Efficiency
EASY-TO-REACH KITCHEN TOOLS

Many cooks keep measuring cups and spoons in a drawer, where they can get buried deep among other utensils. Here's a way to keep these items within easy reach.

Mount a simple hardware-store key holder near your work space, and instead of using it to safeguard keys, hang your measuring cups and spoons from it.

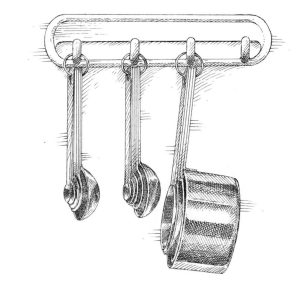

Kitchen Efficiency
CLEAN UTENSILS AT THE READY

Every cook knows the frustration of having to stop in the middle of meal preparation to wash a utensil, such as a paring knife, which you've dirtied but need to use again. Here's how we like to make clean-up quick and convenient.

Fill a large glass or jar with hot, sudsy water. Then, when you dirty a utensil, place it in the glass as soon as you've used it, so that it will need only a quick rinse when you need to reach for it again.

Most home bakers have just one piece of any given type of equipment, such as a strainer or sifter. Of course, these tools must be completely dry before you use them, but waiting for a strainer or sifter to dry fully can be frustrating, and it can't always be accomplished by hand-drying with a dish towel.

Kitchen Efficiency
QUICK DRY FOR BAKING UTENSILS

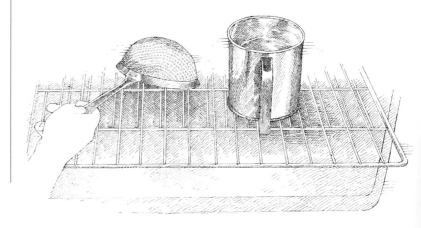

Because the oven is on anyway, put the utensil in it to dry out. Set a timer for about 2 minutes to remind yourself that the utensil is in the oven. Be sure that the utensil doesn't have any plastic parts that can melt. Because the utensil will be quite hot, use a mitt to protect your hand when removing it from the oven.

Kitchen Efficiency
DRYING DISHES QUICKLY

Many cooks who wash dishes by hand would prefer to wash, dry, and put away the dishes in one fell swoop. Using this method, you can get the dishes dry lickety-split without using a dish towel.

Prop a small table fan level with the dishes in the rack and direct the air flow toward the dishes, which will dry in record time.

Kitchen Efficiency
KEEPING DISHES SPOTLESS BETWEEN USES

Many home kitchen pantries, especially the oversized butler's pantries in older houses, feature open storage for platters and serving dishes. The downside of this system is that the open shelves allow the dishes to get dusty between uses. That won't be a problem if you take this precaution.

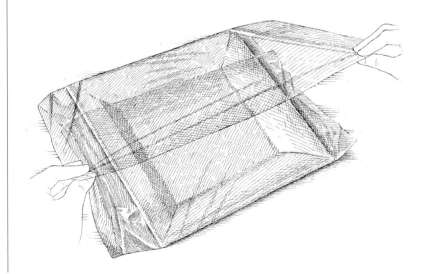

Wrap your dishes tightly with plastic wrap before storing them.

Everyone dreads the huge pile of dishes that builds up after a dinner party
or holiday gathering. In these situations, when the dishwasher and
dish rack are full, drying space can be hard to come by.
Try these two methods to create extra space.

Tip 311

Cooling racks used for
baking are an ideal source of
drying space, especially for
delicate wine glasses. Place a
towel underneath the rack
to absorb the water that
drips off the glasses.

Tip 312

Alternatively, set an oven
rack over the sink. The air
circulating on all sides of the
rack will help dry dishes,
glasses, and other items.

Kitchen Efficiency
WARMING DINNER PLATES

Tip 313

Warm dinner plates make any meal special and are especially welcome in cold winter months. Try this trick for getting all the plates and any serving bowls you need warmed at once.

Run all the plates, platters, and bowls you want to warm through the dishwasher on the dry cycle.

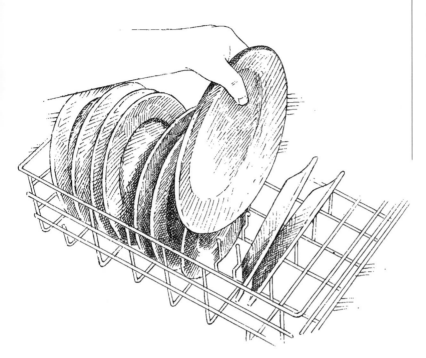

Tip 314

Many cooks enjoy listening to music or watching TV as they cook. But sticky hands can make a real mess on the remote control.

Before cooking, wrap the remote control unit in a layer of clear plastic wrap. The buttons remain visible and operable but don't get smeared by sticky hands.

Kitchen Efficiency
KEEPING THE REMOTE CONTROL CLEAN

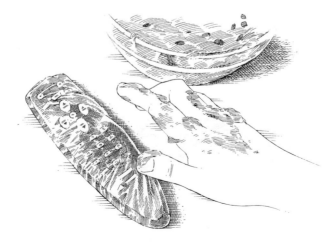

Tip 315

Everyone knows how fat can splatter from a hot skillet. Here's a neat way to sauté and keep the mess under control.

Before you start to cook, lay an overturned baking sheet across the burners next to the pan. The baking sheet, which is easy to clean, catches most of the grease, leaving the burner plates and stovetop relatively free of fat.

Kitchen Efficiency
KEEPING THE STOVETOP CLEAN

Kitchen Efficiency
AN EXTRA-LARGE TRIVET

Tip 316

Many cooks, especially those whose kitchen countertops cannot accommodate hot pots and pans, often have problems finding a spot to put down a hot roasting pan right out of the oven.

To solve this problem, we place an overturned baking sheet on the counter and use it as a trivet on which to rest a hot roasting pan or Dutch oven.

Kitchen Efficiency
CLEANING UP SPILLED OIL

Anyone who has ever dropped a bottle of oil on the floor and had it shatter knows how difficult it can be to clean up. Here's how we deal with an oil-slicked floor in our test kitchen.

❶ Sprinkle a thick layer of flour over the spilled oil and wait a few minutes for the flour to absorb the oil.

With paper towels, or a brush ❷ if there is any glass, move the flour around until it absorbs all the oil, then sweep it up with a dustpan and broom.

❸ Spray the area with window cleaner and wipe away the last traces of oil and flour.

Kitchen Efficiency
MINIMIZE SAUTÉ SPLATTER

Tip 318

When you are browning meat for a soup or stew, grease splatters on the stovetop and burners, resulting in an unpleasant clean-up job. The stovetop is easy to wipe off, but not the burners and burner plates. Here's a way around this chore.

Position inverted disposable aluminum pie plates over the unused burners. The pie plates can be wiped clean and used again.

Tip 319

Kitchen Efficiency
DOUBLE DUTY FOR POT LIDS

Most stews start with browning the meat, which must then be removed from the pan so the other ingredients can be browned, occasioning a dirty dish.

Instead of using a clean dish, invert the lid of the pan in which you're cooking over another bowl or pot. The lid, which you need to wash anyway, now serves as a spoon rest and receptacle for the sautéed food.

Kitchen Efficiency
PAN FLIP THAT STOPS DRIPS

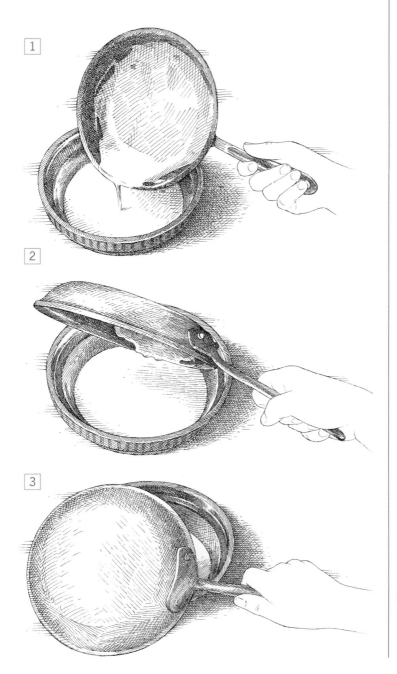

Pouring melted butter, warm oil, sauce, or almost any liquid from a pan often creates a drip down the outside of the pan. This not only makes a mess on the pan's exterior but can burn onto the pan bottom if you place the pan back on a hot burner. Try this the next time the occasion arises.

Instead of immediately turning the pan right side up after pouring out the contents, continue to turn the pan in the direction of the pour, through one full rotation, until it eventually ends right-side up. This forces the liquid to run back into the pan instead of down its side.

Kitchen Efficiency

OPENING TIGHTLY SEALED JARS

Opening a stubborn jar lid sometimes takes a little more than muscle.
Here are four tricks we like.

Tip 321

Drape a piece of plastic wrap over the jar lid for a firm grip.

Tip 322

Rubber kitchen gloves or a rubber band slipped around the lid will also help you get a good grip on a tightly sealed jar.

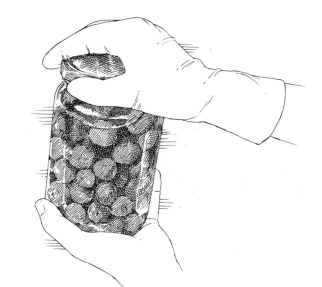

Tip 323

Use a bottle opener to gingerly (so as not to break the glass jar) pry the lid away from the glass to let in air, which breaks the vacuum seal.

Tip 324

Break the vacuum seal of the jar by overturning it in a pie plate filled with hot water. After 30 seconds or so, the heat should break the seal and the lid will unscrew easily.

Kitchen Efficiency
PREVENTING STICKY LIDS

The lids of jars with sticky contents such as jelly or molasses often stick as if cemented in place. Instead of struggling with sticky lids, try one of these tips.

Tip 325

Cover the top of the jar with plastic wrap before screwing on the lid. The plastic prevents any serious sticking, so the lid always unscrews.

Tip 326

Alternatively, dip a small piece of paper towel into a bit of vegetable oil and wipe the threads of the jar. The film of oil will prevent the lid from sticking to the jar the next time you open it.

Tip 327

When the small cap to a bottle of ketchup, Worcestershire or soy sauce, vinegar, or the like sticks and won't unscrew easily, try this method.

Use a nutcracker, which should grip and twist off the cap easily.

Kitchen Efficiency
BOTTLE OPENER AIDE

Tip 328

To get an accurate measurement of water in a liquid measuring cup, you must rest the cup on a flat surface so the water is level. We found this method to be quick, easy, and convenient.

Set a measuring cup next to your kitchen sink and fill it with the sink sprayer.

Kitchen Efficiency
MEASURING WATER ACCURATELY

Kitchen Efficiency
TESTING THE TEMPERATURE OF LEFTOVERS

Judging the interior temperature of reheated leftovers such as lasagna or a casserole can be difficult. To avoid serving leftovers that are tepid in the center, try this method.

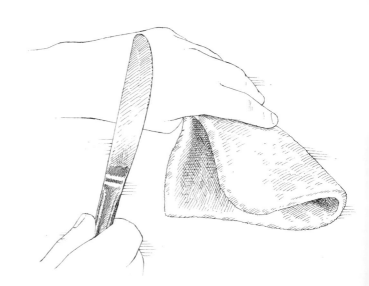

Before taking the casserole ❶ 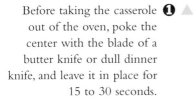 out of the oven, poke the center with the blade of a butter knife or dull dinner knife, and leave it in place for 15 to 30 seconds.

Remove the knife, then ❷ ▶ touch the side of the blade very gently to the back of your hand. If the metal is hot, so, too, is the center of the casserole.

Kitchen Torch
ALTERNATE USES

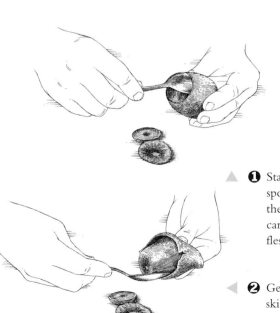

Tip 330

Crème brûlée aficionados use their kitchen torch to caramelize the sugar layer on their favorite dessert, but not for much else.

Get more from your kitchen torch by using it to brown already-baked meringue-topped pies, tartlets, and cakes.

Kiwi
PEELING

Tip 331

A vegetable peeler or knife can be ineffective for removing the hairy skin from a kiwi fruit, tending to crush the soft flesh. We like the following method.

❶ Start by trimming the ends of the fruit. Insert a small spoon between the skin and flesh, with the bowl of the spoon facing the flesh. Push the spoon down and carefully move it around the fruit, separating the flesh from the skin.

❷ Gently remove the spoon and pull the loosened skin away from the flesh.

Don't wait until an
accident occurs to find
out if your knife blade
is dull.

Knives

DETERMINING SHARPNESS

Put your knife to the paper test. Hold a sheet of paper by one end and try slicing clean ribbons from it. If the knife snags or fails to cut the paper, it needs to be steeled or sharpened.

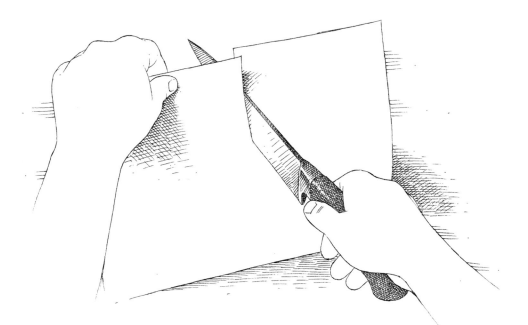

Knives
DETERMINING KNIFE-HONING ANGLE

When honing a knife on a steel or a stone, it's best to hold the blade at a 20-degree angle. But what is a 20-degree angle? Here's an easy way to approximate the angle.

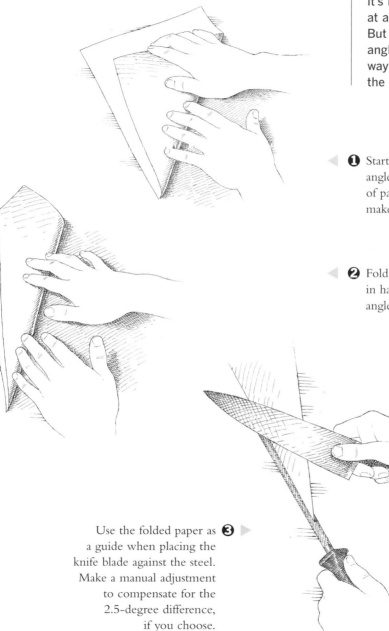

1 Start with the 90-degree angle of a corner of a piece of paper. Fold it in half to make a 45-degree angle.

2 Fold the 45-degree angle in half once more for an angle of 22.5 degrees.

3 Use the folded paper as a guide when placing the knife blade against the steel. Make a manual adjustment to compensate for the 2.5-degree difference, if you choose.

Knives
SAFE KNIFE TRANSPORT

Most home cooks do not have a sheath in which to carry a knife when traveling.
Here are two homemade carriers that work well.

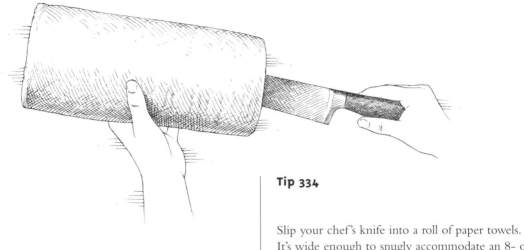

Tip 334

Slip your chef's knife into a roll of paper towels.
It's wide enough to snugly accommodate an 8- or
10-inch knife and if you're off to a picnic, the
paper towels will come in handy.

Tip 335

Cut a slit in a thick piece of
corrugated cardboard and slip
the knife into the opening.

Lasagna — Oysters

Lasagna
MAKING SMALLER BATCHES

Most lasagna recipes produce enough to feed a big crowd, but cooks who are feeding fewer people may not want to make that much.

For single-serve portions, make lasagna in mini-loaf pans. Pans that measure 5¾ by 3 inches are the perfect size for most standard lasagna noodles, which will fit perfectly if cut in half after cooking. The individual loaf pans can be wrapped, frozen, and baked one at a time as needed.

Tips 337 & 338 | **Leeks**
CLEANING

Leeks are often quite dirty and gritty, so they require thorough cleaning.
Both of the following methods require that you first cut the dark green portion into quarters
lengthwise, leaving the root end intact.

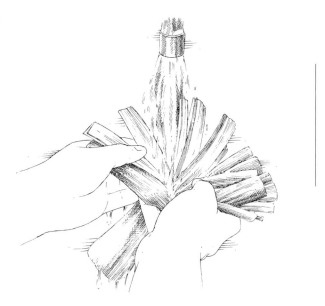

Tip 337

Hold the leek under running
water and shuffle the cut
layers like a deck of cards.

Tip 338

Slosh the cut end of the leek
up and down in fresh, still
water. Repeat as necessary.

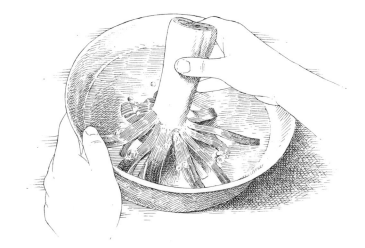

Lemon Slices
FREEZING SLICES FOR BEVERAGES

Lemon slices are a refreshing addition to a glass of water and many other beverages, but if you need just a slice at a time, it can seem a bother. This method makes adding lemon slices to your drink as convenient as adding an ice cube.

Slice a few lemons and lay the slices flat on a parchment-covered baking sheet and freeze, then store frozen in a zipper-lock bag.

Tip 340

Lemons and Limes
SHORTCUT FOR SQUEEZING JUICE

If you need to squeeze a large amount of citrus juice, as when making lemonade or a Key lime pie, try this method.

Place two or three quartered limes or lemons in the hopper of a potato ricer and squeeze the handles together.

Lemon Reamer
IMPROVISE WITH BEATERS

If you find yourself in a kitchen without a citrus reamer, don't despair. This common kitchen tool makes a fine substitute.

A beater from a hand-held mixer can be used to ream lemons beautifully.

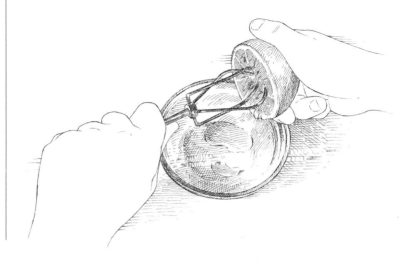

Lemons

REMOVING PEEL FROM A GRATER

Lemon zest often becomes trapped in
the teeth of a box grater and ends up being wasted.
Here are two ways to get around this problem.

Tip 342

Cover the grater with a
piece of waxed paper before
grating. The zest will
remain on top of the waxed
paper rather than clogging
the grater's teeth.

Tip 343

If you don't have waxed paper
on hand, use a toothbrush,
kept especially for this
purpose in the kitchen, to
scrape the trapped zest
off the grater.

Tip 344

Everyone has a trick for juicing lemons. We find that this one extracts the most juice possible from lemons as well as limes.

Lemons
JUICING

Start by rolling the lemon on a hard surface, **❶** ▶
pressing down firmly with the palm of your
hand to break the membranes inside the fruit.

Cut the lemon in half. Use **❷** ▼
a wooden reamer to extract the juice into a
bowl. To catch the seeds, place a mesh strainer
over the bowl.

Lemonade
TWO WAYS TO MASH SLICED LEMONS

We find that sugaring sliced lemons and then mashing them
to release their flavorful oils creates the best lemonade ever. Although you can mash
the sugared lemons with a potato masher or wooden spoon,
here are two ways to work more quickly.

Tip 345

Place the sliced lemons and
sugar in the bowl of a standing mixer
fitted with the paddle attachment.
Turn the mixer to low and mix for
about 45 seconds. (Longer mixing can
mash the lemons too much and make
the lemonade bitter.) To prevent splatters,
drape a kitchen towel over the mixer.

Tip 346

An alternative method is to let sugared
lemon slices macerate for about 15 minutes,
or until softened, and then mash them
in batches with a potato ricer. Set the
ricer right over the lemonade pitcher.

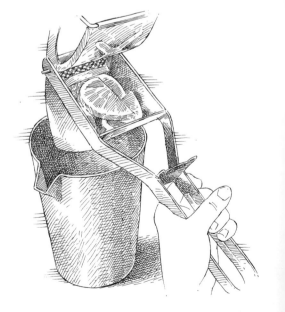

Lemons
FREEZING SPENT SHELLS

Tip 347

Here's a nifty use for the spent shells from juiced lemons and limes.

Place spent shells in a zipper-lock bag in the freezer. When you need acidulated water to hold peeled apples, potatoes, or artichokes, don't waste a fresh lemon—just take a spent shell from the freezer. It has enough juice and acidity to keep these foods from turning brown.

Lemon Grass
BRUISING

Bruising a whole stalk of lemon grass is the best way to release its flavorful juices when infusing a liquid like stock.

Smack the stalk with the back of a large chef's knife and use immediately.

Lemon Grass
MINCING

Tip 349

Because of its tough outer leaves, lemon grass can be difficult to mince. We like this method, which relies on a sharp knife.

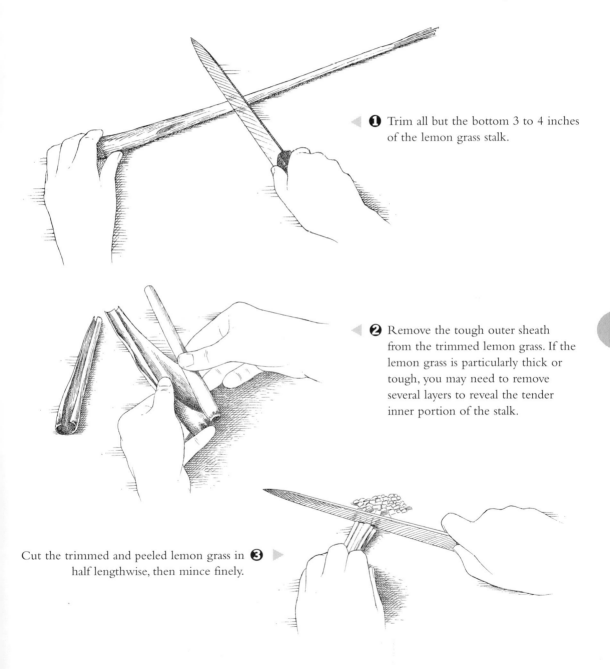

❶ Trim all but the bottom 3 to 4 inches of the lemon grass stalk.

❷ Remove the tough outer sheath from the trimmed lemon grass. If the lemon grass is particularly thick or tough, you may need to remove several layers to reveal the tender inner portion of the stalk.

Cut the trimmed and peeled lemon grass in **❸** half lengthwise, then mince finely.

Lettuce
CORING AND WASHING

Here's a simple way to core and wash a head of iceberg lettuce with just one motion.

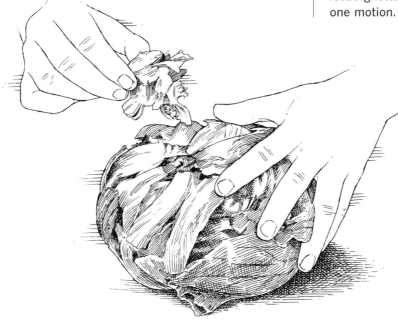

▲ **❶** Rap the bottom of the head of lettuce sharply on the counter to loosen the core. Turn the head of lettuce over and pull out the core in one piece.

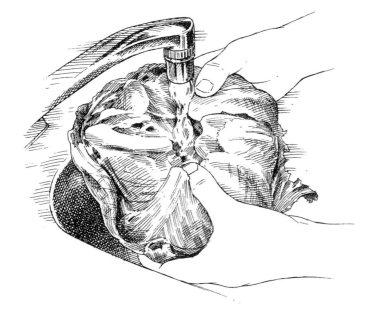

◀ **❷** Fill the hole left by the extracted core with water to rinse soil from the lettuce. Separate the leaves, wash again if necessary, and dry.

Right after molting, a
lobster has a soft shell
that is easy to crack.
However, hard-shelled
lobsters are much
meatier. Here's how
to tell the difference
between the two
stages in the lobster's
life cycle.

Lobsters
DISTINGUISHING HARD-SHELLS FROM SOFT

Squeeze the sides of the lobster's body, just in front of the tail.
A soft-shell lobster will yield to pressure, while a hard-shell lobster
will feel hard and tightly packed with meat.

Lobster
CONTROLLING MESS

Whether eaten at home or in a restaurant, lobster dinners inevitably make a sticky mess when fluid escapes in gushes and geysers from the shells as you crack them to get to the meat. Here's an easy way to stem the tide.

Using tongs, hold the cooked lobster by the tail above the cooking pot, so the claws are pointing down into the pot. Then use kitchen shears to cut about ¼ inch off the tip of each claw and continue holding the lobster as the water in its shell drains back into the pot through the holes in the claws.

Tip 353

Mangoes are notoriously hard to peel, owing to their odd shape and slippery texture. Here's how we handle this tough kitchen task. This method ensures long, attractive strips of fruit.

Mangoes
PEELING

▲ ❶ Start by removing a thin slice from one end of the mango so that it sits flat on a work surface.

Hold the mango cut-side ❷ ▲ down and remove the skin with a sharp paring knife in thin strips, working from top to bottom.

▲ ❸ Cut down along the side of the flat pit to remove the flesh from one side of the mango. Do the same on the other side of the pit.

◀ ❹ Trim around the pit to remove any remaining flesh. The mango flesh can now be chopped or sliced as desired.

Mayonnaise
DRIZZLING IN THE OIL

Tip 354

Homemade mayonnaise is made by slowly whisking oil into beaten egg yolk and lemon juice. It can be difficult to whisk with one hand and pour evenly from a heavy measuring cup with the other hand.

Punch a small hole in the ❶ ▲ bottom of a paper cup.

Whisk the egg yolk and ❷ ▶ lemon juice together and set the bowl on a damp towel. Pour the oil into the cup while holding your finger over the hole, then hold the cup above the bowl and remove your finger to let the oil drizzle in slowly as you whisk.

Measuring Cups
IMPROVISING

If you are cooking in a kitchen without a set of measuring cups, turn to this clever substitution.

Cleaned-out yogurt cups make great homemade measuring cups. Use the 4-ounce size for a ½ cup measure, the 6-ounce size for a ¾ cup measure, and the 8-ounce size for a 1 cup measure.

Roasts cook more evenly when tied at even intervals. Tying also makes the roast more attractive. Here's an easy way to make sure that you space the pieces of kitchen twine evenly.

Meat
SPACING TIES ON A ROAST

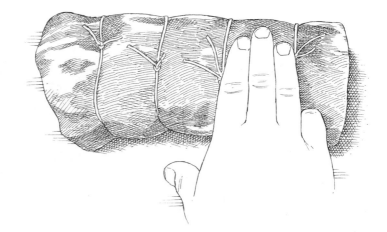

Space the ties about three fingers apart down the entire length of the roast.

Meat
FREEZING FOR EASY SLICING

Tip 357

Many recipes, including stir-fries, soups, and pasta sauces, call for thinly sliced pieces of flank steak, pork tenderloin, or other meats. Here's how to make the slices as thin as possible.

Place the meat in the freezer until partially frozen, 1 to 2 hours, depending on the thickness of the meat. It's much easier to slice through partially frozen meat and turn out thin, even slices.

Tip 358

Roasts and other meats need to rest for several minutes before being carved to give the juices a chance to redistribute throughout the meat, but tenting a roast takes a lot of aluminum foil, which you might not want to spare for this use.

Cover the roast with a large overturned metal bowl.

Meat
KEEPING ROASTS WARM

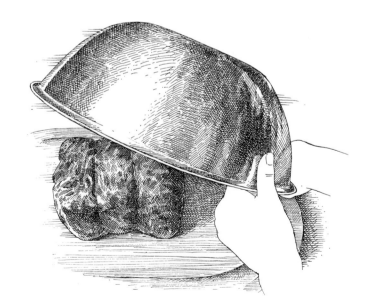

Meat

PROTECTING ROAST CRUST

Tip 359

As your roast rests before carving, don't let the accumulated juices soggy its crusty bottom.

Place the roast on a rack set over a jelly roll or roasting pan, which will keep the roast and its crisp exterior above and away from the dampening juices.

Tip 360

Meat

STEADYING A ROAST FOR CARVING

When carving a roast, it's necessary to steady it, usually with a large fork, but we don't like how it punctures the meat and causes juices to leak. This way keeps the juices inside the meat.

A pair of kitchen tongs grasps a roast or large bird without puncturing the meat.

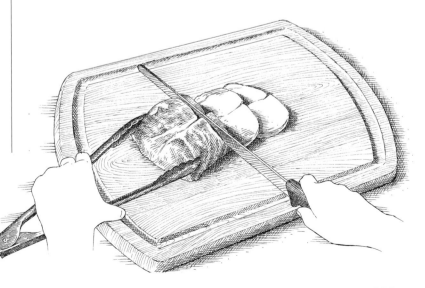

Meat
FREEZING

If you'd like the convenience of pulling out frozen chops, burgers, or steaks as you need them, follow this easy method.

Separate chops, steaks, and burgers with sheets of parchment paper, place the meat in freezer bags, and freeze. The paper makes it much easier to pull individual pieces from the frozen package.

Tip 362

Meatballs must be cooked through and taste best when browned evenly on all sides. Their round shape can make this a challenge.

Once the meatballs have been browned on their two broader sides, use tongs to stand them on the remaining sides to finish cooking. If necessary, lean the meatballs up against one another to get the final sides browned.

Meatballs
ENSURING EVEN BROWNING

Meringue

MAKING ITALIAN MERINGUE

Tip 363

Italian meringue is made with hot sugar syrup, which cooks the egg whites and ensures a stable meringue. If the syrup is allowed to make contact with the metal beater or bowl, it can solidify into small, hard pieces that won't mix with the whites. Here's how to avoid the problem.

Carefully pour the hot sugar syrup into the egg whites, making sure the syrup doesn't touch the metal beater or the sides of the bowl.

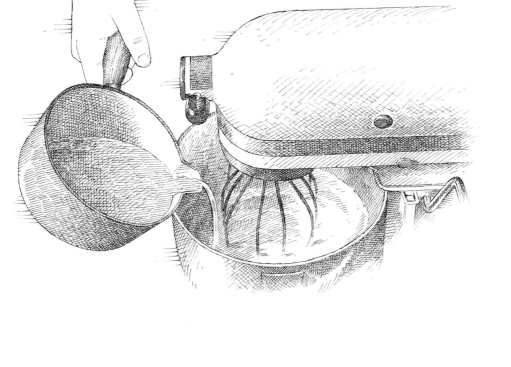

Cleaning dried-on spills
and splatters in your
microwave oven needn't
be a time-consuming
chore.

Microwave Oven
CLEANING

Place a microwave-safe bowl ❶ ▲
full of water in the oven and
heat it on high for 10 minutes.
The steam loosens any dried
food particles, which can then
be wiped off with ease.

▼ ❷ For hard-to-reach corners,
a small disposable foam paint-
brush is just the right size to
brush away any crumbs or
other residue.

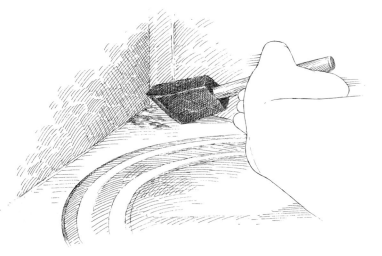

Tip 365

Many recipes call for adding wet and dry ingredients alternately for even blending. Here's how to secure the bowl so you can hold a mixer in one hand and add ingredients with the other.

Mixers *Handheld*
KEEPING BOWLS IN PLACE

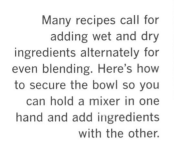

Twist a damp towel to form a ❶ ▷ nest slightly larger than the base of the bowl.

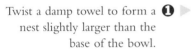

Set the bowl into the nest, ❷ ▽ which will hold the bowl in place as you mix and add ingredients.

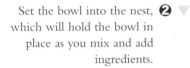

Mixers *Handheld*
SPLATTER-FREE MIXING

Tip 366

Hand-held mixers can get the job done but often cause an excessive amount of splashing, especially when you are beating a thin, liquid batter or whipping cream. Here's how to keep the mess under control.

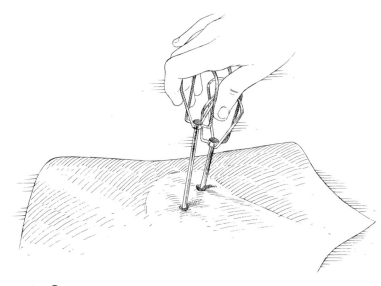

▲ ❶ Take a piece of parchment cut larger than the size of your mixing bowl and make two holes, spaced as far apart as the beater openings on your mixer. Insert the beater stems through the holes and into the beater base.

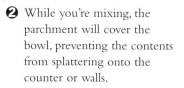

❷ While you're mixing, the parchment will cover the bowl, preventing the contents from splattering onto the counter or walls.

Mixers *Standing*
MOVING HEAVY MIXERS

Tip 367

Many standing mixers, as well as food processors, are heavy and don't slide easily. They can be difficult for many people to lift. Here's a good way to move them around the counter with ease.

Place your mixer on a towel or cloth placemat, which then can be pulled anywhere on the counter with little effort.

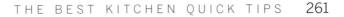

Mixers *Standing*
KEEPING THE MESS UNDER CONTROL

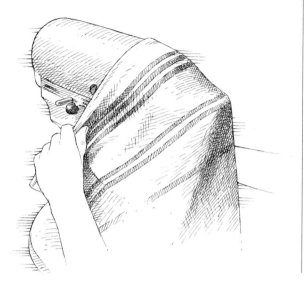

Dry ingredients can puff out in a cloud of fine particles when mixed, while wet ingredients, such as cream or liquid batters, can splatter. Here's a good way to keep your counter clean when using a standing mixer.

Once the ingredients are in the bowl, drape a clean, very damp dish towel over the front of the mixer and bowl. Draw the towel snug with one hand and then turn on the mixer. When done, simply wash the towel.

Mortar and Pestle
IMPROVISING WITH A COFFEE MUG

Mortars and pestles are great for grinding chiles, spices, nuts, or even herbs. Many modern kitchens are not equipped with this tool, however. Here's how to make a mortar and pestle with objects likely to be found in any kitchen.

Place the ingredients to be ground in a shallow, diner-style stoneware coffee cup (which will be the mortar), and use a heavy glass spice bottle as the pestle.

Sometimes muffins will
stubbornly stick in the
pan. Here's a way to pry
them out with little
likelihood of tearing
the muffin apart.

The thin, slightly curved
blade of a grapefruit knife is
particularly suited to getting
under a stubborn muffin with
little chance of damage.

Muffins
LIBERATING TRAPPED MUFFINS

Mushrooms
FLAVORING PORTOBELLOS

Tip 371

Big, meaty portobello caps can be studded with garlic and herbs, just like a piece of meat.

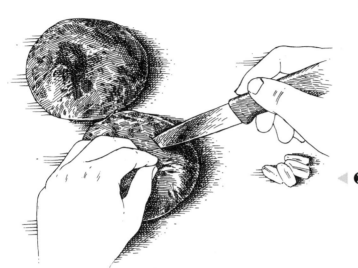

❶ Use the tip of a paring knife to make 10 or 12 narrow slits in the top of each portobello cap.

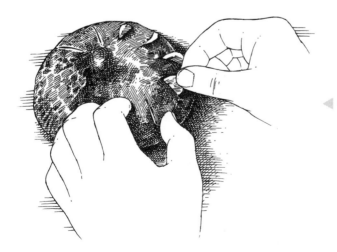

❷ Insert a sliver of garlic into each slit along with a sage leaf, some fresh rosemary, or maybe a tiny sprig of thyme. The garlic and herbs will remain inside the portobello as it cooks.

Mushrooms
SLICING BUTTONS QUICKLY

Slicing button mushrooms thinly takes some patience. Here's a novel way to speed up the process.

Trim a thin piece from the stem end of each mushroom, then cut the trimmed mushrooms, one at a time, in an egg slicer. The pieces will be even and thin.

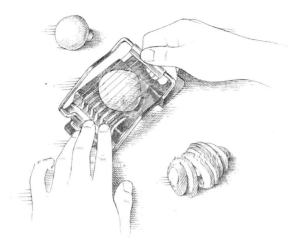

Mushrooms
GRILLING BUTTONS

Once the mushrooms have been cleaned and any dry ends trimmed from the stems, slide each one onto a skewer through the stem up through the cap. This will make the mushrooms less likely to rotate on the grill, so they can be turned easily for even cooking.

Grilling gives white button mushrooms a rich brown crust and meaty flavor. Proper skewering keeps them from falling through the grill grate and allows for even grilling.

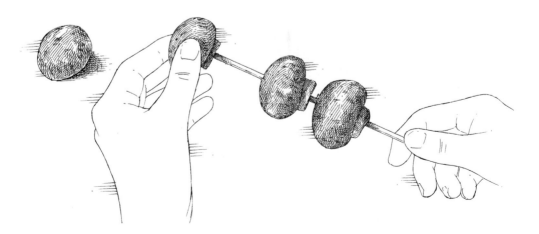

Mushrooms
SOAKING DRIED PORCINI

Dried porcini, as well as shiitakes, oysters, and other dried mushrooms, must be reconstituted before being added to recipes. Soak the porcini in hot tap water (about 1 cup per ounce of dried mushrooms) in a small bowl until softened, about 20 minutes. Here's how to make sure any sand or dirt released by the mushrooms doesn't end up in your food.

❶ Most of the sand and dirt will fall to the bottom of the bowl, so use a fork to lift the rehydrated mushrooms from the liquid without stirring up the sand.

❷ Never discard the flavorful soaking liquid, which can be added to soups, sauces, rice dishes, or pasta sauces. To remove the grit, pour the liquid through a small sieve lined with a single sheet of paper towel and placed over a measuring cup.

Mussels
DEBEARDING

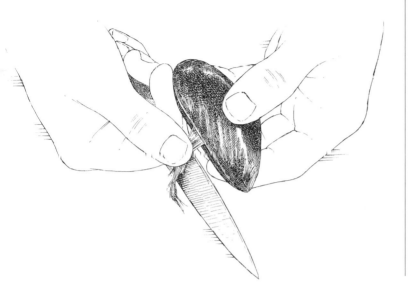

Mussels often contain a weedy beard protruding from the crack between the two shells. It's fairly small and can be difficult to tug out of place. Here's how we handle this task.

Trap the beard between the side of a small knife and your thumb and pull to remove it. The flat surface of the paring knife gives you some leverage to extract the pesky beard.

Nuts
CHOPPING QUICKLY

Chopping a large batch of nuts can be a tedious task. Here's how to speed up the process.

Place the nuts on a cutting board and hold two chef's knives parallel to each other in one hand and chop. Use the other hand to guide the knives through the nuts.

Nuts
CHOPPING NEATLY

Tip 377

Chopping hazelnuts or peanuts can sometimes mean a wild chase around the cutting board as the nuts roll every which way. Here is an easy way to contain the nuts.

Wet a kitchen towel (or two, ❶ ▽ depending on how many nuts you have to chop), grasp both ends, and twist them in opposite directions to form a tight rope.

▽ ❷ Lay the rope on the board in a ring around the nuts. Leave enough room in the center of the ring to fit the knife, and chop away.

Oil

POURING SMOOTHLY

Many households buy olive oil in gallon containers, pouring some into a smaller can or bottle for daily use. But pouring from such a huge container can be a problem, especially when the oil glugs and sloshes out.

❶ To even out the flow while pouring, use a can opener to punch a hole in the top of the container opposite the pouring spout.

❷ Having thus evened out the pressure in the container, you can pour the oil in a smooth, continuous flow.

The sugar content of Vidalia, Walla Walla, and Maui onions, which is what endears them to many cooks, also makes them spoil more quickly if they are stored touching each other. Here's how to prolong their freshness.

Place one onion in the leg of an old but clean pair of pantyhose. Tie a knot in the hose, just above the onion. Repeat this process up the entire leg of the pantyhose.

Onions
STORING VIDALIAS

Onions
KEEPING ONIONS ORGANIZED

It's always best to use up onions that have been sitting in the pantry before breaking into a fresh supply. But it's difficult to keep track of the older versus the younger onions.

Using a permanent marker, lightly mark a small **X** on the skin of each onion now in your storage bin. Leave any new onions you add to the bin unmarked, so that you'll know to reach for the marked onions first. When all of the marked onions have been used, mark the remaining.

Mincing onions can be tedious work, but take heart—there are shortcuts. This one is the easiest we've come across.

Onions
MINCING WITH EASE

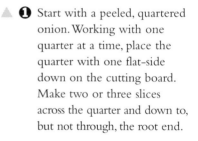

❶ Start with a peeled, quartered onion. Working with one quarter at a time, place the quarter with one flat-side down on the cutting board. Make two or three slices across the quarter and down to, but not through, the root end.

❷ Turn the quarter onto its other flat side and repeat the slicing.

❸ Using the claw grip, with your fingertips folded inward toward your palm to hold the onion in place, cut across the existing slices to make an even dice.

Onions
GRILLING RINGS

Onion slices can be difficult to handle on the grill, with rings often slipping through the grate and onto the coals. Here's how to grill onions safely and easily.

❶ Cut thick slices (at least ½ inch) from large red, Vidalia, or Spanish onions and impale them all the way through with a slender bamboo skewer (it should be about the same thickness as a toothpick or a thin metal skewer). If using longer skewers, thread two slices on each skewer.

❷ The skewered onion slices remain intact as they grill so no rings can fall onto the coals. Best of all, the onions are easily flipped with tongs.

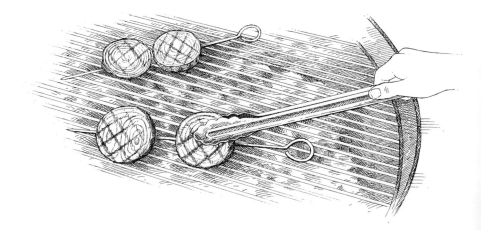

Orange Juice
SHORTCUTTING FROZEN JUICE PREPARATION

When the craving for orange juice hits, waiting for a can of frozen concentrate to thaw before mixing it with water can be frustrating. Here's a way to avoid the wait.

❶ Run the can of frozen concentrate under hot water so it will melt just enough to release from the can.

❷ Use an immersion blender to mix the still-frozen block of concentrate with water. The action of the blender produces a smooth, lump-free juice—with no waiting.

Oranges
REMOVING SEGMENTS

When presentation matters, you will want to remove segments from an orange without any white pith or membranes. Use the same technique with grapefruit.

Start by slicing a small ❶ section, about ½ inch thick, off the top and bottom ends.

With the fruit resting flat, ❷ use a sharp paring knife to slice off the rind and the bitter white pith. Slide the knife edge from top to bottom, closely following the outline of the fruit to minimize waste.

Working over a bowl to catch ❸ the juice, slip the blade between a membrane and a section and slice to the center, separating one side of the section.

Turn the blade so that it is ❹ facing out and is lined up along the membrane on the opposite side of the section. Slide the blade from the center out along the membrane to free the section. Continue until all the sections are removed.

Oven Thermometer
RETRIEVING

Tip 385

Oven thermometers are apt to fall off the rack and onto the oven floor. Retrieval can be a difficult proposition, especially with a hand protected by a bulky oven mitt.

Use a pair of tongs to retrieve or reposition the thermometer. Tongs keep your hands a safe distance away from the hot rack while enabling dexterity that's not possible with your hand clad in an oven mitt.

An oyster knife with a slightly angled, pointed tip is the best tool for opening oysters. The long blade can also be used to detach the oyster meat from the shell.

Oysters
SHUCKING

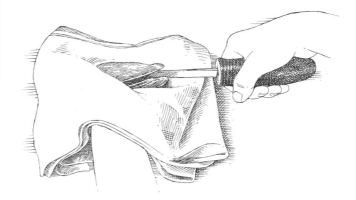

❶ Start by holding the oyster cupped-side down in a kitchen towel. (The towel is essential because it will protect your hand in case the knife slips.) Make sure to keep the oyster flat as you work, to keep the flavorful juices from spilling out of the shell. With the tip of the knife, locate the hinge that connects the top and bottom shells. Push between the edges of the shells, wiggling the knife back and forth to pry them open.

❷ Detach the meat from the top shell and discard the shell.

❸ To make eating easier, sever the muscle that holds the oyster meat to the bottom shell.

Pancakes – Poultry

Pancakes
KEEPING THEM WARM

Pancakes are best eaten as soon as they come off the griddle. Of course, this isn't always possible. Here's how to keep them warm for a few minutes while you round up the troops.

Place the pancakes on a platter lined with a clean cloth napkin or tea towel. Pull the towel over the pancakes and then cover with an inverted colander to keep them warm.

Pan Drippings
EASY DEFATTING

Tip 388

No one looks forward to spooning that thin layer of liquid fat off the drippings from a roast before making a pan sauce or gravy. Yet if the fat remains, the sauce will be greasy. Here's a method that makes the process faster and easier.

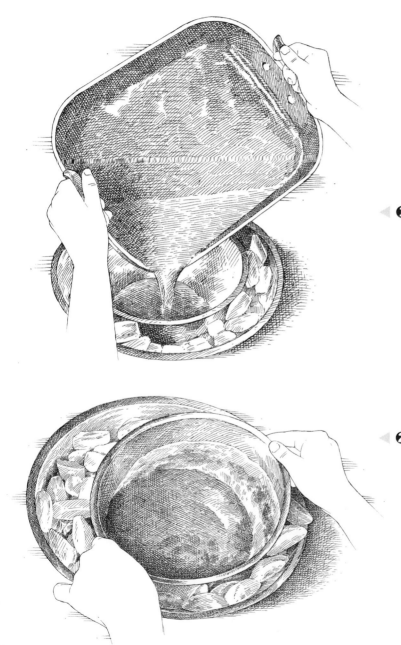

❶ Deglaze the roasting pan, fat and all, and scrape up and dissolve the brown bits from the bottom of the pan, but stop short of reducing the liquid. Pour the brown, fatty liquid into a small mixing bowl (metal works best because it reacts quickly to changes in temperature), and set the bowl in an ice water bath.

❷ After a few minutes, as the liquid cools, small bits of fat will solidify and rise to the surface. If you rock the inner bowl very gently to create a small wave of liquid moving around its perimeter, the fat will collect around the upper inside edge of the bowl, where it will be easy to remove.

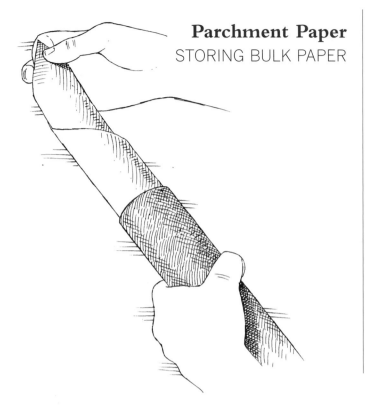

Parchment Paper
STORING BULK PAPER

Tip 389

Parchment paper is a must for many baking projects. To save money, we like to buy it in bulk in sheets (rather than in rolls), but storing a large quantity can be a challenge. Here's how to keep parchment safe and out of the way.

Roll a quantity of parchment paper sheets into a tight roll and slide it inside an empty gift-wrap tube, which can be stored in the pantry or kitchen. The sheets can be pulled out easily, one at a time.

Tip 390

Parsley
STORING

Chopped parsley is an easy, attractive garnish for many dishes, but it's a nuisance to chop at the very last minute, when you've got steaming-hot plates of food to serve to hungry guests waiting at the table.

Chop the parsley finely, then ❶ ▷ place it in the center of a clean kitchen towel.

In that last flurry of activity before saucing pasta and getting dinner on the table, it's easy to overlook small details. It's no wonder, then, that many cooks forget to save a bit of pasta cooking water to add to the sauce when the recipe recommends it. Try this foolproof reminder.

Pasta *Draining*
RESERVING PASTA WATER

Before cooking the pasta, set up the colander for draining it in the sink, then place a measuring cup inside the colander. It's sure to nudge your memory at the appropriate moment.

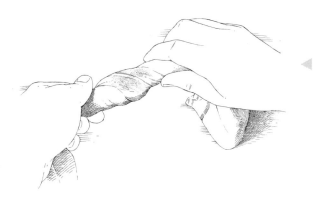

❷ Wrap the towel around the parsley, and then twist both ends very, very tightly, until you see green parsley juice bleeding through the cloth. Twist as tightly as you can to extract as much juice as possible. The dried parsley will stay fresh-looking for hours.

Tip 392

Even when drained well in a colander, the curved shape of macaroni and other similar-shaped pasta tends to hold in some cooking water. To thoroughly dry cooked macaroni and prevent the excess water from diluting your pasta salad dressing, we recommend this method.

Pasta *Draining*
FOR SALAD

❶ After shaking the macaroni dry in a colander, spread it in an even layer on a rimmed baking sheet lined with paper towels. Let the macaroni dry for 3 minutes.

❷ Roll the macaroni in the paper towels to blot any remaining moisture, then transfer the macaroni to a bowl.

You don't need a fancy
pasta rack to dry pasta.

Hang the pasta over the
bars of a wooden indoor
adjustable clothes rack.

Pasta
DRYING FRESH PASTA

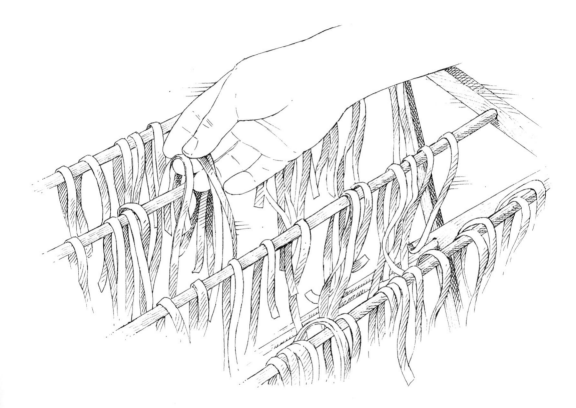

It's always easier to fill a
pastry bag when it is
propped up and open.

Pastry Bag
FILLING THE BAG

Roll down the top of the pastry bag and, depending on the size of the
bag, fit it into a Pilsner beer glass, blender jar, or Pringles potato chip
can. Fold the cuff at the top of the bag over the top edge, and spoon the
frosting down into the bottom of the bag, which is held snugly in place.

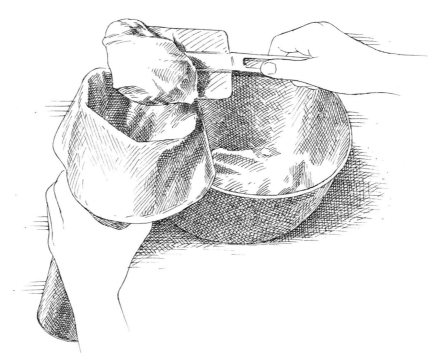

Pastry Cream
QUICK COOLING

Pastry cream and puddings come off the stove hot but must be cooled to room temperature, or even chilled, before they can be used. By maximizing the surface area from which steam can escape, you will speed up the process.

❶ Spread the pastry cream or pudding across a rimmed baking sheet that has been covered with plastic wrap.

❷ Once the pastry cream or pudding has been spread to the edges of the pan, cover it with another piece of wrap to keep a skin from forming. Snip a number of holes in the plastic wrap to allow steam to escape.

Peaches
REMOVING THE PIT

Tip 396

If you're tired of wrestling with peaches and nectarines to remove the pit, try this method, in which the peach splits neatly so the pit can be removed.

Locate the crease that marks **❶** ▲ the pointed edge of the pit.

❷ Position the knife at a 90-degree angle to the crease and cut the fruit in half, pole to pole.

❸ Grasp both halves of the fruit and twist apart. The halves will come apart cleanly, without splitting, so the pit can be easily removed.

Peaches
PEELING

Some recipes, especially for pies, call for peeled peaches. A vegetable peeler often mashes the fruit, while a knife trims a lot of edible flesh with the skin. Use this method instead, which also works with nectarines.

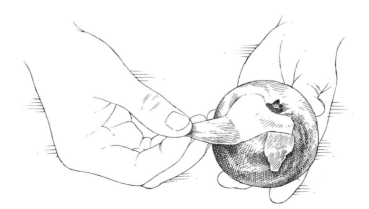

Bring a small saucepan of water to a boil. Add the **❶** ▲ peaches and simmer, turning once or twice, for 30 seconds. Use a slotted spoon or mesh skimmer to transfer the peaches to a bowl of ice water to stop the cooking process.

▼ **❷** When cool enough to handle, remove the peaches from the water and slip off the skins with your fingers.

Peanut Butter
BLENDING NATURAL BUTTERS

Fans of natural peanut butter (without sugar or other stabilizers), tahini, and other nut butters know that the butter often separates into a dense, solid mass beneath a layer of oil that has risen to the surface. Before spreading, the oil and the solids have to be reblended. A spoon makes a mess of everything. Try one of these tricks instead.

Tip 398

Turn the sealed jar upside down and allow the oil to rise again to the top. As the oil passes through the nut butter, the solids will absorb some oil and become soft enough to spread. Flip the jar right-side up, and the nut butter is ready to use.

Tip 399

Scrape the contents of the jar into a wide food storage container (such as Tupperware) and then mix very well. The extra space allows for mixing without splashing oil, and mixing vigorously and completely keep the oil and butter blended. It also allows you to easily mix in a sweetener, such as honey, if you desire.

Pears
CORING

We find that pears really should be cut in half to get at the core.

1

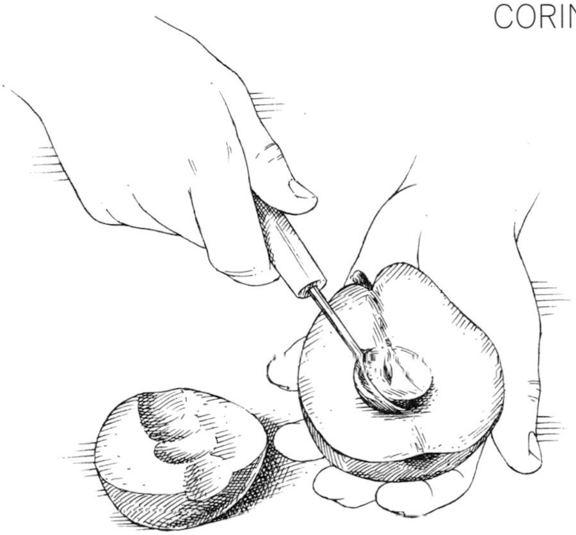

2

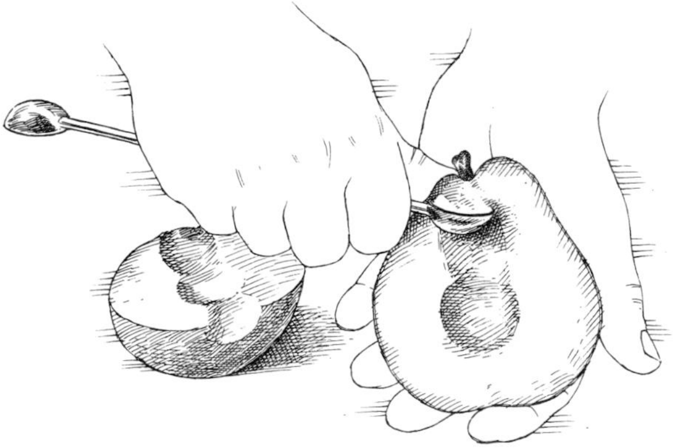

3

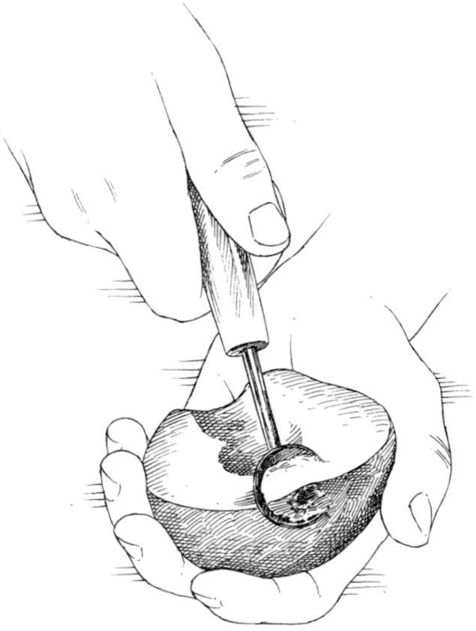

❶ Use a melon baller to cut around the central core with a circular motion.

❷ Draw the melon baller from the central core to the top of the pear, removing the interior portion of the stem as you go.

❸ Use the melon baller to remove the blossom end as well.

Peppercorns
TWO WAYS TO CRUSH PEPPERCORNS

For recipes requiring crushed peppercorns, such as steak au poivre, where the pepper forms a crust, it's important that the peppercorns be coarsely crushed. Some households might not have an adjustable pepper grinder with a coarse setting. In that case, try these methods, often used by restaurant chefs.

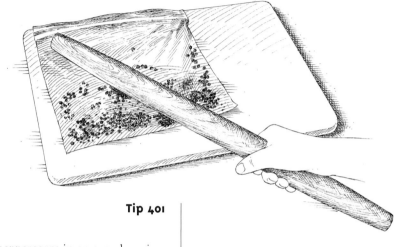

Tip 401

Spread the peppercorns in an even layer in a zipper-lock plastic bag and whack them with a rolling pin or meat pounder.

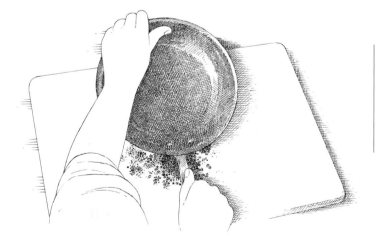

Tip 402

Use the back of a heavy pan and a rocking motion to grind the peppercorns.

Peppercorns
GRINDING LARGE AMOUNTS

At one time or another, many cooks face the task of seasoning a huge quantity of meat with salt and ground black pepper while preparing for a large dinner party or big outdoor barbecue. Before you break a sweat, try this powerful alternative.

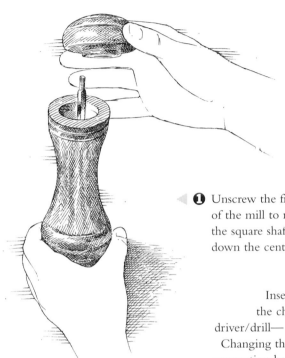

❶ Unscrew the finial at the top of the mill to reveal the tip of the square shaft that runs down the center.

Insert the shaft into **❷** the chuck of a power driver/drill— and off you go. Changing the tension in the connection between shaft and driver/drill controls the grind size, from fine to coarse.

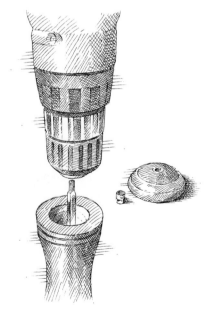

Pepper Mill
JAM-FREE LOADING

Anyone who has filled a pepper mill using a funnel knows how frustrating it is when the peppercorns jam in the neck.

Cut off the bottom of a small plastic soda or water bottle whose neck is small enough to fit easily into the mouth of a pepper mill but is wider than a funnel neck, so no jamming will occur.

Pepper Mill
KEEPING THE GRINDER CLEAN

Preparing raw cutlets, ground meat, or poultry for cooking can leave the cook's hands greasy and slippery when it is time to season the meat. Here's how to grind fresh pepper over meats, even when your hands are dirty.

Before you handle the meat, drape a small piece of plastic wrap over the pepper mill. Your hand touches only the plastic, which can be removed and discarded once the meat has been seasoned.

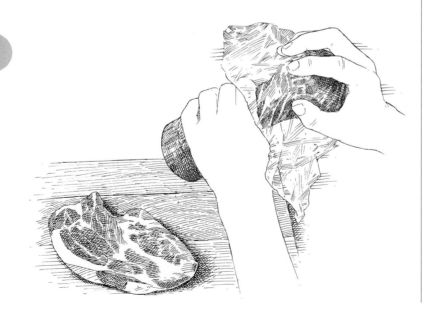

Pepper Mill
PREVENTING A PEPPERY MESS

Cooks who use a mill to grind their own pepper know that even the best mill invariably leaves a mess of ground pepper on the surface where it is set down. Here's how to avoid this nuisance and capture every last bit of pepper from your grinder.

When you're done using the mill, set it in a small ceramic dish, such as a ramekin or Japanese soy sauce dish. Excess pepper ends up in the dish, not on the counter, and can even be collected, measured, and used for cooking.

Peppers
ROASTING

Most recipes instruct the cook to roast whole peppers under the broiler until blackened. The uneven shape of a bell pepper means that one part always burns while another remains undercooked. We prefer to flatten the peppers before roasting, which lets them cook evenly and makes them much easier to peel. As an added bonus, the seeds can be removed before roasting, not after, when your hands are slippery and the seeds stick to everything.

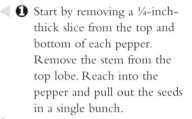

❶ Start by removing a ¼-inch-thick slice from the top and bottom of each pepper. Remove the stem from the top lobe. Reach into the pepper and pull out the seeds in a single bunch.

❷ Slit through one side of the pepper, then lay it flat, skin side down. Slide a sharp knife along the inside of the pepper to remove all the white ribs and any remaining seeds.

Arrange the flattened peppers **❸** ▲ and the top and bottom pieces, all skin-side up, on a baking sheet lined with foil. Flatten the strips with the palm of your hand.

Roast the peppers under the **❹** ▶ broiler until the skins are charred but the flesh is still firm. Wrap the pan tightly with foil and steam the peppers to help loosen the skins. When the peppers are cool enough to handle, peel off the skin in large strips.

Peppers *Stuffed*
KEEPING UPRIGHT

Cooks who've made stuffed bell peppers know they have an annoying tendency to topple toward disaster in the roasting pan. Here are a few solutions.

Tip 408

Reserve the tops of the peppers—which you have cut off to open the peppers for stuffing—and insert them between the stuffed peppers for added stability.

Tip 409

Instead of cooking the peppers in a baking dish or roasting pan, as specified in most recipes, place them in a tube pan. The snug fit makes the peppers sit upright.

Tip 410

Alternatively, place the peppers in the cups of a muffin tin, whose cups hold the peppers firmly in place.

Tip 411

Place each pepper in an individual ovenproof ramekin or custard cup. This is also a great system when you want to cook only a couple of peppers, instead of a whole batch.

Pressing graham cracker
crumbs into a pie plate
can be a messy
proposition, especially
when the buttered and
sugared crumbs stick
to your hands.

Keep the crumbs where they
belong by sheathing your
hand in a plastic sandwich
bag and pressing the crumbs
firmly but neatly.

Pies *Crumb Crusts*
PRESSING CRUMBS INTO PLACE

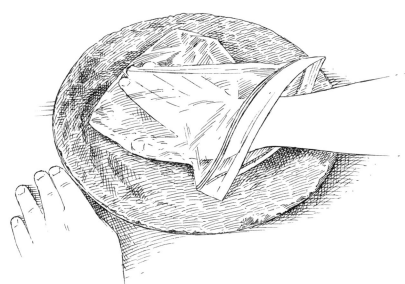

Pies *Dough*
ADDING ICE WATER

Most pie pastry recipes use ice water to bring the dough together. However, if you add too much water, the dough can become mushy. Instead of sprinkling water, one tablespoon at a time, over the dough, try this method, which also guarantees properly chilled water.

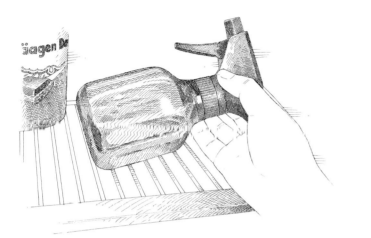

Fill a spraybottle with about ❶ ▲
¼ cup water and store it on
its side in the freezer.

▲ ❷ When you're making pastry, grab the bottle from the freezer and fill it with cold water, which quickly chills on contact with the ice in the bottle. Spray ice water over your pastry mixture as needed. This method ensures that the water is evenly distributed over the flour mixture, making it unlikely that you will add too much.

Pies *Dough*
MAKESHIFT ROLLING PIN

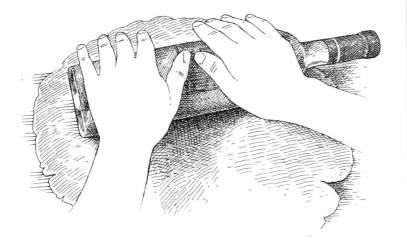

Tip 414

We find that a tapered wooden pin does the best job of rolling out pie pastry. But here's a way to roll out dough when a pin is nowhere to be found.

An unopened wine bottle has the right weight and shape for rolling out dough. If possible, use white wine and chill the bottle. The cold temperature of the bottle will help keep the butter in the dough chilled.

Tip 415

It seems that no matter how much you flour the counter, pie dough often sticks as you roll it out. Adding more flour isn't the solution and can actually make the dough tough.

Instead, slide a bench scraper (also called a pastry scraper) under the dough every 30 seconds or so. This way the dough never has a chance to stick, and it won't tear when you need to move it. If you don't own a bench scraper, use a metal spatula in the same fashion.

Pies *Dough*
PREVENTING STICKING

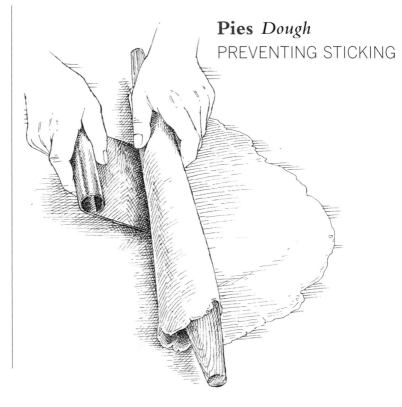

Pies *Dough*
MEASURING THE DOUGH

Tip 416

There's nothing worse than transferring the rolled dough to a pie plate only to realize you haven't rolled it large enough. Here's an easy way to measure the dough as you work.

Invert the pie plate over the dough. There should be an inch or two of extra dough on all sides of the pie plate.

Tip 417

Pies *Dough*
MOVING THE DOUGH

Once the dough has been rolled out evenly, it must be transferred to the pie plate. This is how we like to accomplish this delicate task.

Work a bench scraper or thin metal spatula under the dough, then roll the dough onto the rolling pin (see tip on facing page). Move the pin over to the pie plate and gently unroll the dough over the filling.

Pies *Dough*
CUTTING AWAY EXTRA DOUGH

Tip 418

Excess dough must be trimmed so that you can fashion a neat edge for the pie.

We find that kitchen shears make the best tool for slicing away extra dough. Leave about ½ inch of dough hanging over the rim of the pie plate so you have something to flute.

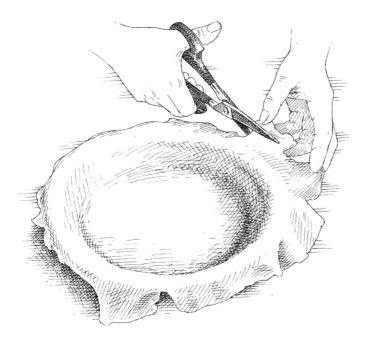

Tip 419

To create a fluted edge around the exterior of the pie, you need a sturdy, thick piece of dough.

Fold the excess dough back under itself, pressing it firmly to seal. This double-thick edge can be fluted or decorated as desired.

Pies *Dough*
FOLDING EXCESS DOUGH UNDER

Tip 420

A fluted edge makes a pie especially attractive. It also helps to contain the filling.

Hold the inside of the dough with the thumb and forefinger of one hand and press the outside of the dough with the forefinger of the other hand.

Pies *Dough*
FLUTING THE EDGE

Pies *Weights*
EFFICIENCY

Streamline your pie-making efforts by using this all-in-one pie weight storage and lining method.

Store your pie weights in a doubled-up ovenproof cooking bag, which you can simply lift in and out of the pie plate and use over and over, eliminating the extra step of lining the pie crust with parchment or foil.

Pies *Weights*
IMPROVISING

We prefer ceramic or metal pie weights but if you have neither, try this substitution.

Pennies, which conduct heat beautifully, also lie flat and thus make formidable pie weights.

Pies
EASY, EVEN LATTICE

A lattice top crust on pie makes an attractive presentation, but achieving strips of dough of even lengths and widths can pose a problem.

Use a thin, inch-wide metal ruler to line up both the length and width of the lattice.

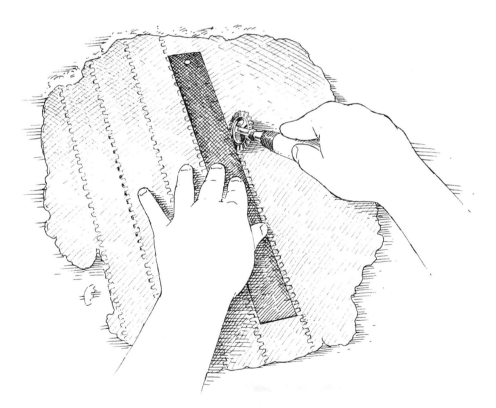

Pies *Dough*
PROTECTING THE RIM

The fluted edge on a pie can burn in the oven because it's so exposed. Many recipes suggest piecing together strips of foil to fashion a protective cover for the edge. Instead of trying to twist pieces of foil together, we prefer to use a single sheet to cover the pie edge.

❶ Lay out a square of foil slightly larger than the pie. Fold the square in half to form a rectangle. Cut an arc that is roughly half the size of the pie.

❷ When you unfold the foil, you will have cut out a circle from the middle of the sheet. This open circle exposes the filling, while the surrounding foil covers the crust.

Pies

APPLYING A MERINGUE TOPPING

A meringue topping that is uneven or has shrunk back around the edges of the pie is disappointing. Here's how to get an even meringue topping that covers the entire surface of the pie.

❶ Put dabs of meringue over the filling.

❷ Once all the meringue has been placed on the pie, use a rubber spatula to "anchor" the meringue to the edge of the crust. As long as the meringue touches the crust, it won't pull away or shrink in the oven.

The whipped cream or meringue topping on a pie can be marred easily when covered directly with plastic wrap.

To keep the surface of your pie neat, stand a few strands of uncooked spaghetti or linguine in the pie and suspend a sheet of plastic wrap over the pasta. Don't try this with toothpicks, which are likely to sink down into the pie.

Pies *Cream*
SAFE TRANSPORTING

Pineapple
PREPARING

A pineapple can seem daunting to peel and core. We find that the following method is easy and reliable.

Start by trimming the ends of ❶ the pineapple so it will sit flat on a work surface. Cut the pineapple through the ends into four quarters.

Place each quarter, cut-side ❷ up, on a work surface, and slide a knife between the skin and flesh to remove the skin.

❸ Stand each peeled quarter on end and slice off the portion of tough, light-colored core attached to the inside of the piece. The peeled and cored pineapple can be sliced as desired.

Pine Nuts
TOASTING EVENLY

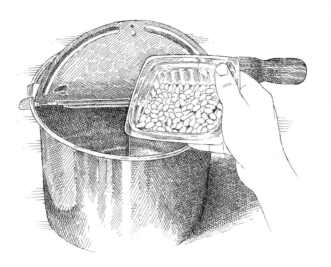

Pine nuts are difficult to toast evenly on the stovetop. Because of their shape, they tend to rest on one side and are prone to burning.

We find that a hand-cranked stovetop popcorn popper is the perfect vessel for toasting pine nuts. Just heat the popper, add the nuts, and then use the crank to keep the nuts in constant motion until they are evenly toasted.

Homemade pizza is a blank canvas for the creative use of toppings. The problem is that you don't always have enough topping options on hand. Here's a simple way to create interesting pizzas.

Whenever you are cooking something that would make a good pizza topping, reserve a little bit in a clean, plastic container, label it, and freeze it. When making pizza, sort through the frozen topping options.

Pizza
KEEPING TOPPINGS ON HAND

Pizza
DRIER TOMATO TOPPING

Don't let juicy tomatoes make your pizza crust soggy.

Place fresh tomato slices in a salad spinner and spin dry.

Pizza
CLEAN REMOVAL FROM PIZZA PEEL

Getting a sticky pizza dough to slide off a pizza peel can be tricky. We like this method, which relies on parchment paper.

Roll out and sauce the pizza on parchment paper. You can then slide the pizza, paper and all, onto the peel and into and out of the oven with ease. The parchment won't burn, and it easily slides off the peel.

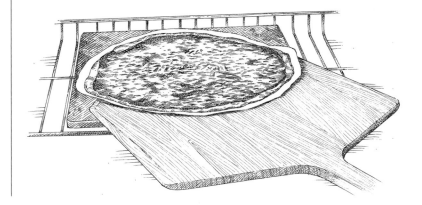

Pizza *Grilled*
GETTING TOPPINGS HOT

Tip 432

Grilled pizza is delicious, but often the crust starts to burn on the bottom before the toppings are hot. It's imperative to top grilled pizzas very lightly and use ingredients that will cook quickly. Here's a good way to ensure that the toppings get nice and hot.

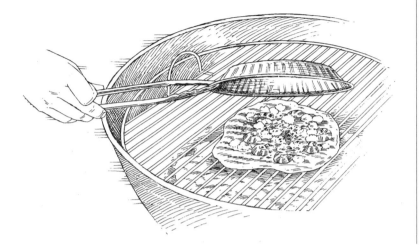

Once the toppings have been applied, invert a disposable aluminum pie plate over the pizza. The pie plate traps heat and creates an ovenlike effect.

Tip 433

It can be hard to tell when a deep-dish pizza is done, especially if cheese and toppings are obscuring the crust. Just because the toppings are sizzling doesn't mean the crust is cooked through.

Pizza *Deep-Dish*
DETERMINING WHEN IT'S DONE

Use a spatula to lift up the pizza slightly. If the bottom crust is nicely browned, the pizza is done.

Tip 434

When cutting pizza, a regular knife can catch and drag the melted cheese, and pizza wheels often dent the pan when you bear down to cut through the crust.

A pair of kitchen shears cuts through pizza easily. Just hold the edge with a folded paper towel to pick up the crust for an easier cutting angle.

Pizza
CUTTING WITH SCISSORS

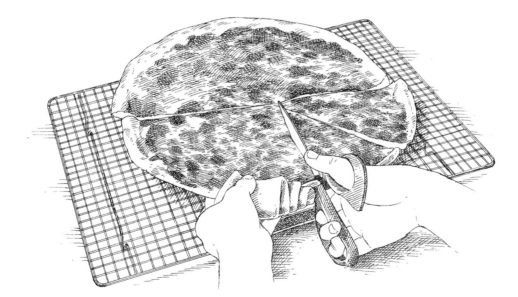

Polenta
PREVENTING LUMPS

Lumpy polenta is not very appealing. Here is the best way to ensure a smooth porridge.

When the water comes to a boil, pour the polenta into the water in a very slow stream from a measuring cup, all the while stirring in a circular motion with a wooden spoon to prevent clumping.

Polenta
SMOOTHING OUT THE LUMPS

Even if you add the cornmeal to the water in a slow, steady stream, your polenta might have tiny lumps in it. Here's how to get rid of the lumps and produce perfectly smooth polenta.

Once the polenta has finished cooking, use an immersion blender to smooth out any lumps. The blender can also be used to help incorporate butter, cheese, or herbs added just before serving.

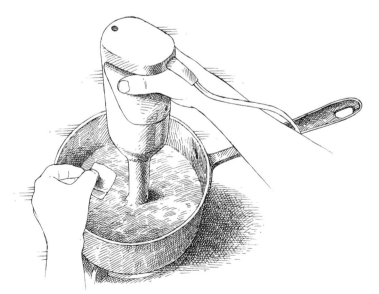

Pork
KEBABS

Pork, especially smaller pieces like those for kebabs, can easily dry out on the grill. This method, using butterflied pieces of boneless center-cut pork chops, guarantees maximum surface area when marinating for moist, tasty meat.

Cut the boneless pork chops into 1 ¼-inch cubes, then cut each cube almost through at the center to butterfly before marinating.

Pork Tenderloin
REMOVING THE SILVER SKIN

The tenderloin is covered with a thin membrane called the silver skin. When heated, the silver skin shrinks and can cause the tenderloin to bow and thus cook unevenly. Here's how to remove the silver skin before cooking.

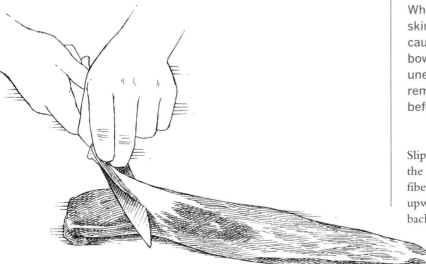

Slip a paring knife between the silver skin and the muscle fibers. Angle the knife slightly upward and use a gentle back-and-forth sawing action.

Pork Tenderloin
SLICING FOR STIR-FRIES

Tip 439

Our favorite cut of pork for stir-frying is the tenderloin, which is lean and tender. Here's how we get thin, even strips from this long piece of meat.

❶ Freeze the tenderloin until firm, 1 to 2 hours. Cut the tenderloin crosswise into ⅓-inch-thick medallions.

❷ Slice each medallion into ⅓-inch-wide strips.

Potatoes
SCRUBBING CLEAN

Recipes in which the potatoes are not peeled usually instruct the cook to "scrub" the potatoes. This same technique is used with other root vegetables that will be cooked with the skin on, such as turnips, carrots, beets, and sweet potatoes. Here's a quick and easy way to loosen dirt from the exterior of potatoes and other root vegetables.

Buy a rough-textured bathing or exfoliating bath glove especially for use in the kitchen. The glove cleans away dirt but is relatively gentle and won't scrub away the potato skin.

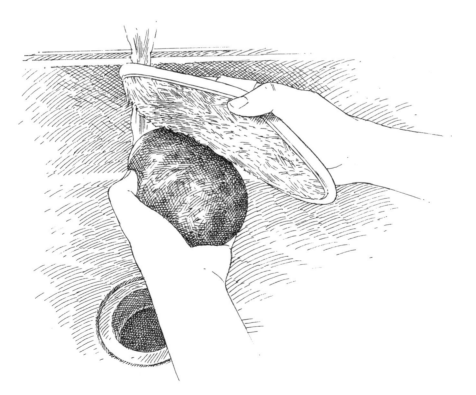

Potatoes
DRYING BOILED

Tip 441

Shaking just-boiled potatoes gently in the hot pan after pouring off the water is a common method of drying them a little before seasoning and dressing them. But it's all too easy to break the potatoes apart his way. Try this method instead, making sure to set the pan on a cool burner or trivet.

❶ After pouring off the water, cover the pot with a clean dish or tea towel.

❷ Replace the pot lid. After a minute or two, the towel will have absorbed the excess moisture from the potatoes.

Potatoes
EASIER PEELING

Peeling the skin from a slippery potato can result in scraped fingers or a dropped potato. Equally frustrating is trying to peel a hot cooked potato held in an oven mitt. Here are two ways (one for raw potatoes, one for cooked) to make this task easier.

Tip 442

When peeling a raw potato, insert a corkscrew, which will hold the potato in place and give you a handle to grip.

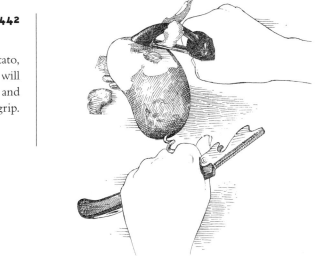

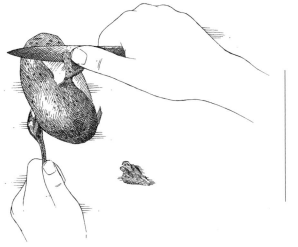

Tip 443

Spear a hot potato with a fork, then hold onto the fork with one hand and peel the potato with the other.

Potatoes *Mashed*
SHORTCUT

When potatoes are destined for mashing, we prefer to boil them with their skins on to keep them from getting waterlogged. There is no doubt, though, that peeling just-boiled potatoes can be a painstaking job. Try this trick to skip a step.

Tip 444

Cut each potato in half and place cut-side down in a ricer. This way the flesh is forced through the holes while the skin remains in the hopper.

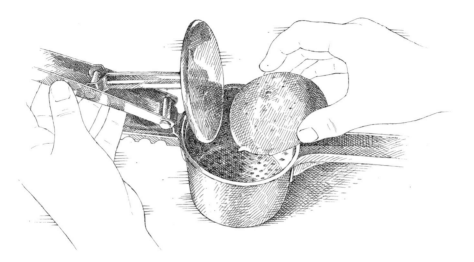

Tip 445

It's always nice to serve food from a warm dish, but it's particularly nice with mashed potatoes, which otherwise cool quickly.

Potatoes *Mashed*
WARMING SERVING BOWL

Drain the water in which the potatoes have boiled into the serving bowl. While you mash potatoes, the heat from the water will warm the bowl. Be sure the bowl you use is heatproof.

Tip 446

For the best results, bake potatoes in a 350-degree oven until tender, about 75 minutes. To ensure that the flesh does not steam and become dense, it's imperative to open up each baked potato as soon as it comes out of the oven. This technique maximizes the amount of steam released and keeps the potato fluffy and light.

Potatoes
OPENING A BAKED POTATO

❶ Use the tines of a fork to make a dotted **X** on top of each baked potato.

❷ Press in at the ends of the potato to push the flesh up and out. Besides releasing steam quickly, this method helps the potato trap and hold onto bits of butter.

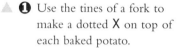

Potatoes

FOLDING HASH BROWNS

The best hash browns have as much potato crunch as possible. Removing excess water from the grated potatoes before cooking will help them crisp up in the pan. This folding technique ensures that every bite is packed with crunch.

Once the potatoes have been browned on both sides, fold the cake over, omelet style. When cut into wedges, each piece will now have four crisp surfaces—two inside and two outside.

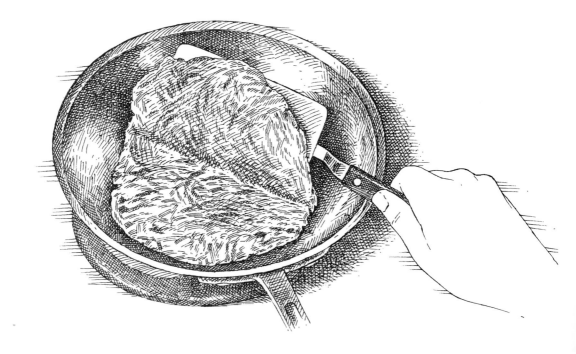

The starchy, thick-skinned russet is the potato of choice when it comes to steak fries. The following technique ensures uniform wedges for even cooking.

Potatoes

CUTTING FOR STEAK FRIES

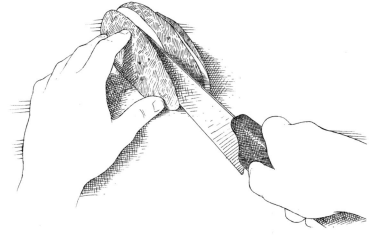

Cut each potato in half ❶ ▷ lengthwise. Place the potato half flat-side down and cut into thirds lengthwise.

◁ ❷ Cut each piece of potato in half lengthwise to yield 12 wedges that measure ¾ inch across on the skin side.

Poultry
RINSING BRINED POULTRY

Brining chicken or turkey produces a moist, well-seasoned bird, but rinsing the excess salt off the surface can make a soggy mess of your countertop. Here's a way to streamline the process.

Place the chicken or turkey ❶ ▷ on a wire rack. Set the rack in an empty sink, and use the sink sprayer to wash off the meat. Then blot the meat dry with paper towels.

If you plan to air-dry the ❷ ▽ chicken or turkey, simply set the rack with the towel-dried pieces on a rimmed baking sheet or jelly roll pan and place the whole thing in the refrigerator.

Ravioli – Stuffing

Ravioli
IMPROMPTU WRAPPERS

Tip 450

Store-bought wonton wrappers can be used as a substitute for homemade pasta when making ravioli.

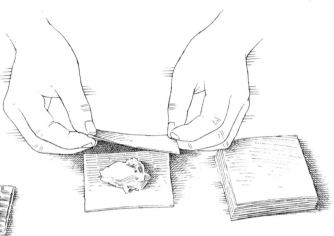

▲ ❶ Place one wrapper on a work surface. Spoon some homemade filling on top. Brush the edges of the wrapper with a little water, and then cover with a second wrapper.

▼ ❷ Use the tines of a fork to seal shut the edges of the ravioli. Make sure that the seal is tight so that the filling won't leak out while the ravioli are being cooked

Recipes
PROTECTING IN THE KITCHEN

To protect recipes from the splotches and splatters of
usual kitchen duty, many cooks use plastic page protectors, available
at office supply stores. These common household items
can also do the job.

Tip 451

Place a zipper-lock bag flat
on the counter, slide the sheet
of paper right into it, and zip
shut. Gallon-sized bags work
nicely for 8½ by 11-inch
sheets, while sandwich-sized
bags work nicely for
newspaper recipes mounted
on index cards.

Tip 452

Clean, dry glass pot lids also
do the job. Place the lid over
the sheet of paper, or even
over an open cookbook or
magazine. The weight of the
lid will keep the pages open.

Rhubarb

PEELING

Rhubarb stalks, especially thick ones, are covered with a stringy outside layer that should be removed before cooking. Make sure to cut away and discard the leaves, which are inedible.

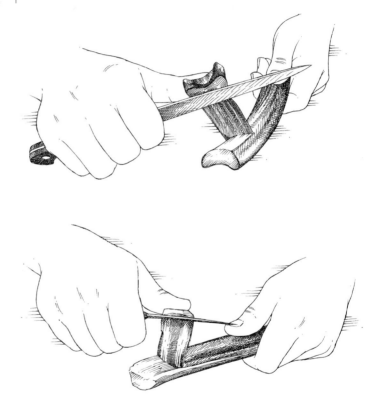

❶ Trim both ends of the stalk. Partially slice a thin disk from the bottom of the trimmed stalk, being careful not to cut all the way through. Gently pull the partially attached disk away from the stalk, pull back the outer peel, and discard.

❷ Make a second cut partially through the bottom of the stalk in the reverse direction. Pull back the peel on the other side of the stalk and discard. The rhubarb is now ready to be sliced or chopped as needed.

Whether cooking regular
rice or making pilaf, we
find that a dry, fluffy
texture is best.

Rice
STEAMING FOR FLUFFY TEXTURE

Once the rice is tender, remove the pan from the heat, place
a clean kitchen towel folded in half over the saucepan, replace the lid,
and set aside for 10 minutes. Residual heat continues to steam the
rice and improves its texture, while the towel absorbs excess moisture
that would otherwise condense on the lid and eventually fall
back into the rice and make it mushy.

When rinsing rice prior to cooking, it can be tricky to pour off the water without sending some of the rice down the drain. Here are two different methods that tackle this problem.

Tip 455

Place the rice on a splatter screen. Use the sink sprayer to rinse the rice through the screen. This method works best with smaller amounts of rice.

Tip 456

Pour the rice in a wire mesh strainer or colander, and then set the strainer into a large, water-filled bowl. When you're done soaking, simply lift out the strainer and let the rice drain.

Saffron
CRUMBLING TO RELEASE FLAVOR

Saffron is the world's most expensive spice, so you certainly want to extract every drop of flavor. Here's how to get the most bang for your buck.

Before adding saffron to a stew or soup, crumble the threads between your fingers to break up the saffron. Crumbling releases flavorful oils and helps the saffron dissolve in the liquid.

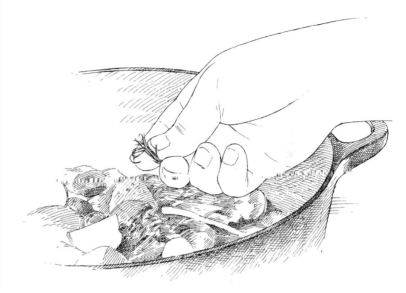

Salad Spinners
GETTING BETTER LEVERAGE

Salad spinners with a top-mounted turn crank can rumble and vibrate during use. Here's how to make the spinning go more smoothly.

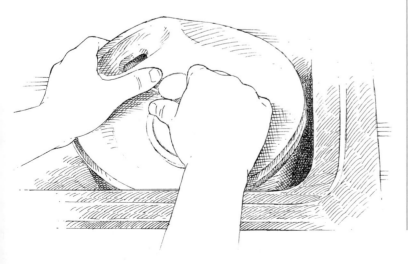

Place the salad spinner in the corner of your sink. This increases your leverage by lowering the height of the crank. This extra leverage also acts to push the spinner down to the sink floor and into its walls, stabilizing it.

Salad Spinners
SPINNING GREENS DRIER

Salad spinners go a long way toward drying clean, wet salad greens, yet greens sometimes need a post-spin blot with paper towels before they are tossed into a salad bowl. Try this all-in-one method for drier greens in no time.

Combine the two steps by spinning two or three paper towels in with the greens.

Locating and removing the pinbones from a side of salmon can be tricky. Running your fingers along the flesh is one way to locate them. This way is even better.

Invert a size-appropriate mixing bowl on a work surface and drape the salmon over it, flesh-side up. The curve of the bowl forces the pinbones to stick up and out, so they are easier to spot, grasp with pliers, and remove.

Salmon
REMOVING PIN BONES FROM A SIDE OF SALMON

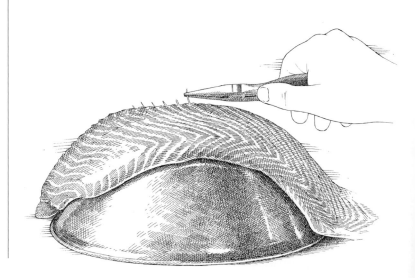

Salmon
REMOVING PINBONES FROM FILLETS

Salmon fillets will occasionally contain a few tiny white pinbones. These bones are smaller and thinner than a toothpick and can be hard to find.

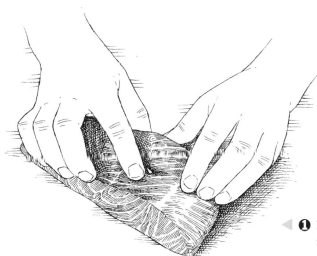

❶ Before cooking, rub the tips of your fingers gently over the surface of each salmon fillet to locate any pinbones. They will feel like small bumps.

❷ If you find any bones, use a clean pair of needle-nose pliers or tweezers to pull out the bones.

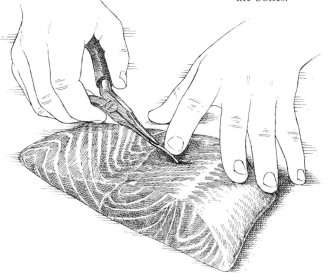

Salmon
TURNING A FILLET INTO STEAK

Many people prefer fillets to steaks because they would rather not deal with the bones. But because they are thinner at the edges, salmon fillets do not cook evenly. Some people may like the gradation from well-done at the edges to rare in the center, but others may not. Steaks have a consistent thickness and cook evenly from edge to edge. Here's a neat way to turn a fillet into a boneless steak.

❶ Start by cutting lengthwise through a 3-inch-wide fillet down to, but not through, the skin.

❷ Fold out the two flesh pieces, with the skin acting as a hinge.

A 3-inch-wide fillet will now ❸ look like a steak, but without any bones, and have an even thickness of 1½ inches. The cooking time for mock steaks is the same as for regular fillets. The one drawback to this method is that the skin won't crisp because it is sandwiched in the middle of the steak.

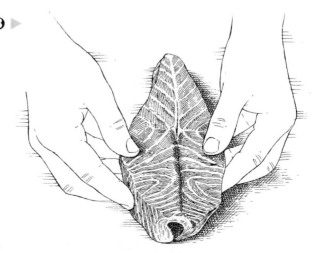

Fiddling with the sharp, pesky metal spouts on boxes of kosher salt or dishwasher soap powder to open them can lead to both general irritation and broken or scratched nails. Make the task easier with this trick.

Salt
EASY PULL-TABS FOR SALT BOXES

Attach a small piece of **❶** Scotch or masking tape to the tip of the pouring spout.

❷ The tape becomes a pull-tab that's easy to grasp.

Salt
PREVENTING CLUMPS

Cooks who live in hot, humid climates know that salt often clumps in the shaker, making it difficult to sprinkle onto foods at the table.

Add a few grains of uncooked rice to the shaker. The rice will absorb excess moisture and keep the salt crystals from clumping together.

Sandwiches
STABILIZING OVERSTUFFED SANDWICHES

Overstuffed sandwiches like hoagies, grinders, or subs can pose a messy problem when the filling spills out every which way.

Remove some of the interior crumb from the top and bottom halves of the bread. This creates a trough in the bottom half for the fillings and a cap on the top for toppings.

Sandwiches
MAKESHIFT SANDWICH PRESS

Toasted, pressed sandwiches such as croque monsieur, cubano, or grilled cheese with embellishments like ham or roasted peppers take on a dense, luxurious texture and a deep even crust when weighted in the pan or on the griddle with a heavy, cast-iron sandwich press. If you don't own a press, don't despair.

Fill a tea kettle with water and use it to weigh down the sandwiches as they cook. If you prefer, fill a saucepan with water and use it in the same manner. Remember to wipe the kettle or pan bottom before its next use.

Sauces and Stocks
ACCURATE REDUCTION

Before making your sauce, place enough water in a sauce pan to equal the volume of the reduced sauce. Place a clean metal ruler into the water and note the mark the water reaches. Empty the pan to prepare the sauce. Periodically dip the ruler into the sauce to see if the sauce has reduced to the right level.

Tip 467

When reducing a liquid for a sauce or stock, it can be difficult to accurately determine when the liquid has reduced to the desired amount. This method is a surefire way to get an accurate read.

Sauces and Stocks
DEFATTING

Although overnight refrigeration is the best way to defat a stock or sauce, here is a method that works well for defatting liquids while they're still warm.

Allow the liquid to cool just ❶ ▷ slightly and then place it in a large, heavy-duty zipper-lock bag. Seal the bag and allow enough time for the fat to rise to the surface of the liquid.

Hold the bag by one of the ❷ ▽ top corners and cut off the point of one of the bottom corners to act as a spout. As soon as the liquid is drained, pinch the spout to capture the fat in the bag.

Scallions
SLICING WITH SCISSORS

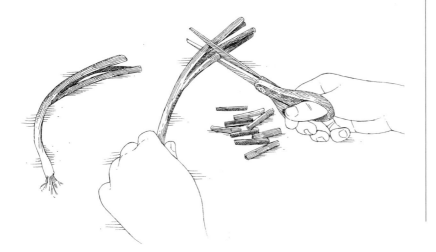

Slicing or chopping scallions with a knife often crushes their natural tube shape and spoils their appearance. Use this method with scallions as well as chives.

Starting at the green end, use scissors to cut neat, intact pieces of scallion.

The small, rough-textured, crescent-shaped muscle that attaches the scallop to the shell often is not removed during processing. It will toughen if heated and should be removed before cooking.

With your fingertips, gently peel away a single tendon from the side of each scallop.

Scallops
REMOVING TENDONS

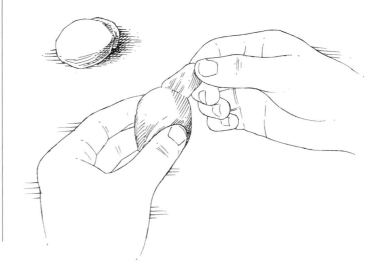

Scallops
GRILLING

To promote browning when grilling scallops, skewer them. This also make it easier to turn many scallops at one time.

Thread the scallops onto doubled skewers so that the flat sides of each scallop will rest on the cooking grate. To turn the skewers, gently hold one scallop with a pair of tongs and flip.

Shallots
MINCING

There are several ways to mince a shallot. We like this technique, which also works with garlic.

❶ Place the peeled bulb flat-side down on a work surface and slice crosswise almost to (but not through) the root end.

❷ Make a number of parallel cuts through the top of the shallot down to the work surface.

❸ Finally, make very thin slices perpendicular to the lengthwise cuts made in step 2.

Many pie bakers have experienced the frustration of trying to clean measuring cups that have contained a solid fat such as shortening or lard. Here's a good way to avoid the mess.

Shortening
MESS-FREE MEASURING CUPS

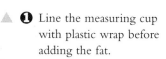

❶ Line the measuring cup with plastic wrap before adding the fat.

❷ Push the fat into the cup with a spatula or wooden spoon to be sure the cup is completely full.

❸ When you remove the fat, the measuring cup stays clean. You can wrap the fat in the plastic to chill it before cutting it into the flour for the pie dough.

Shrimp
DEVEINING WITH SHELLS ON

When cooked by dry heat (pan-searing or grilling), shrimp are best left in their shells. The shells hold in moisture and flavor the shrimp as they cook. However, eating shrimp cooked in their shells can be a challenge. Slitting the shells before cooking is a good compromise—the shrimp are easy to peel at the table, but the flesh is protected as they cook.

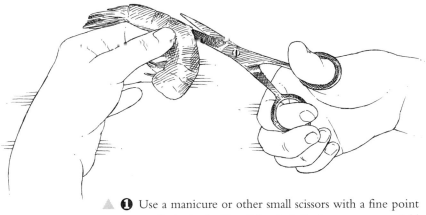

▲ **❶** Use a manicure or other small scissors with a fine point to slit the back side of the shell. Each person can quickly and easily peel away the shell after the shrimp are cooked.

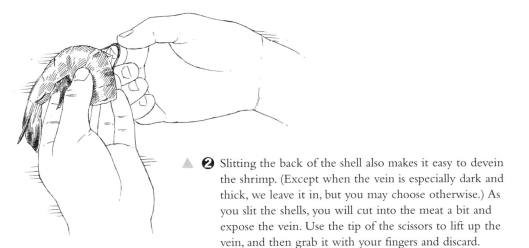

▲ **❷** Slitting the back of the shell also makes it easy to devein the shrimp. (Except when the vein is especially dark and thick, we leave it in, but you may choose otherwise.) As you slit the shells, you will cut into the meat a bit and expose the vein. Use the tip of the scissors to lift up the vein, and then grab it with your fingers and discard.

Shrimp
GRILLING

Shrimp should be skewered before grilling to keep them from falling through the grate. However, every cook has been frustrated by shrimp that spin around on skewers and are impossible to turn.

❶ Thread the shrimp by passing the skewer through the body near the tail, folding the shrimp over, and passing the skewer through the shrimp again near the head.

❷ Long-handled tongs make it easy to turn hot skewers on the grill. Lightly grab onto a single shrimp to turn the entire skewer.

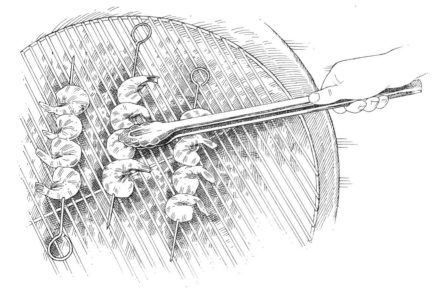

Tip 476

Stuffed snow peas make
tasty and attractive hors
d'oeuvres. Neatly opening
each pod, however, can be
tiresome. This method
streamlines the process.

A seam ripper is the perfect
tool for opening the pods
neatly and quickly.

Snowpeas
OPENING NEATLY

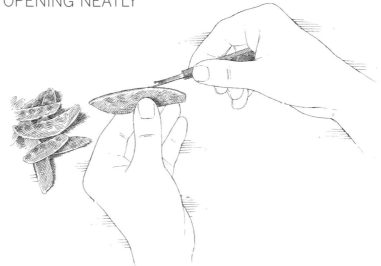

Tip 477

Here's an easy way to
keep drips and spills to a
minimum when ladling
soups or stews.

Before lifting the filled ladle
up and out of the pot, dip the
bottom back into the pot, so
the liquid comes about
halfway up the ladle. The
tension on the surface of the
soup grabs any drips and pulls
them back into the pot.

Soups
DRIP-FREE LADLING

Soups
QUICK-CHILLING

Soups and stews often taste best the day after they are made. They should be cooled to room temperature before being refrigerated. However, if you cook in the evening, this can mean waiting up until the wee hours just to get the soup in the refrigerator. Here's a quick way to bring down the temperature of a hot pot of soup or stew.

Fill a large plastic beverage bottle almost to the top with water, seal it, and freeze it. Use the frozen bottle to stir the soup or stew in the pot; the ice inside the bottle will cool down the soup or stew rapidly without diluting it.

Tip 479

Homemade soup is a winter treat that's easy to freeze, but most people freeze it in large, multiserving portions that make for a lot of unnecessary defrosting when the need for just one or two servings arises.

Soups
FREEZING IN SINGLE-SERVING PORTIONS

Set out a number of 10- or 12-ounce paper cups for **❶** △ hot beverages and fill each with a portion of cooled soup (but not all the way to the top). Label, wrap in plastic wrap, and freeze each cup.

Whenever you want a quick **❷** ▷ cup of soup, remove as many servings as necessary from the freezer and microwave them until they're hot.

Soups *Stock*
STRAINING OUT SOLIDS

Tip 480

Once you have simmered chicken backs or fish heads to make stock, it can be cumbersome to strain out the solids. The solids can splash, and you risk losing a fair amount of liquid in the process.

We use a large pot with a pasta insert to make stock. When the solids have given up their flavor, simply lift the insert and its cargo out of the pot easily and neatly. For clarity, the remaining liquid should be strained, but without any large solids in the pot this job is much easier and neater.

Many recipes call for small amounts of stock. Instead of defrosting a large container of home-made stock just to get a cup or two, you can freeze stock in small portions.

Soups *Stock*
FREEZING IN CONVENIENT PORTIONS

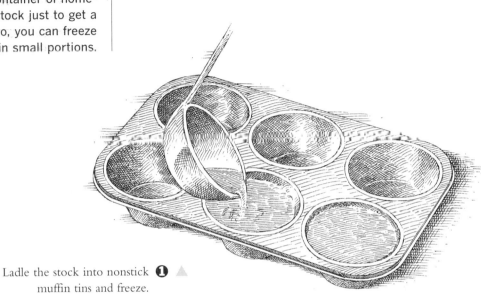

Ladle the stock into nonstick **❶** ▲
muffin tins and freeze.

▼ **❷** When the stock is frozen, twist the muffin tin in the same manner you twist an ice tray, tapping the bottom with a knife to loosen if necessary. Place the frozen blocks in a zipper-lock plastic bag, seal tightly, and use as needed.

Soups *Stock*

FREEZING IN PLASTIC POUCHES

Here's another good way to freeze stock in small portions. Stock frozen this way takes up very little room in the freezer.

❶ Line a coffee mug with a quart-sized plastic zipper-lock bag. (This keeps the bag open so both hands will be free for pouring.)

❷ Fill the bag almost to the top with room temperature stock and seal it. Repeat until all the stock has been placed in bags.

Stack the bags flat in a large, shallow **❸** roasting pan and freeze. Once the stock is solidly frozen, the bags can be removed from the pan and stored in the freezer wherever there's room.

Spaghetti

BREAKING LONG PASTA STRANDS NEATLY

Broken spaghetti or linguine is used in some casseroles, such as turkey Tetrazzini. Here's a tidy way to break spaghetti strands in half.

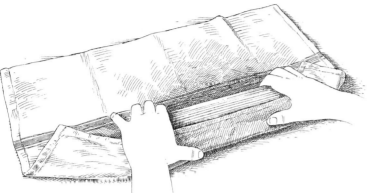

▲ ❶ Roll up the bundle of spaghetti in a kitchen towel that overlaps the pasta by 3 or 4 inches at both ends.

▼ ❷ Holding both ends firmly, center the rolled bundle over the edge of a table or counter. Push down with both hands to break the pasta in the middle of the bundle.

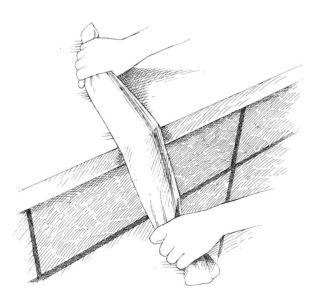

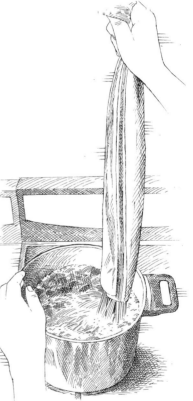

▲ ❸ Holding the bundle vertically over the pot of boiling water, release the bottom of the cloth so that the pasta slides neatly into the pot.

It can be frustrating to sort through a drawerful of spice bottles, lifting and replacing each one, to find what you are looking for. Here's a better way to find spices and keep track of their age.

Spices
STORING EFFICIENTLY

❶ Using stick-on dots, write the name and purchase date on the lids of spice jars when you bring them home from the market.

It is easy to locate and extract **❷** the spice you want and to know when a spice is past its prime and should be replaced. Dry spices should be discarded after one year.

Spices
MEASURING NEATLY

Measuring spices can be tricky, especially if measuring spoons won't fit into narrow bottles. Also, many cooks measure spices right over the mixing bowl, which can lead to overspicing of foods. Here's how we measure spices, leaveners, and salt in our test kitchen.

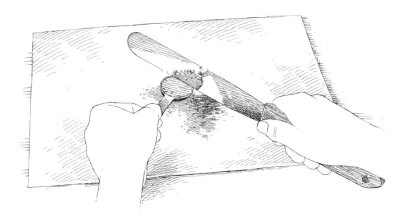

1 Working over a sheet of parchment paper, wax paper, or paper towel, fill the measuring spoon, mounding excess spice over the spoon. With a flat spatula, sweep off the excess onto the paper below.

Add the measured spice to **2** the mixing bowl, then fold the paper in half and slide the excess spice back into the bottle.

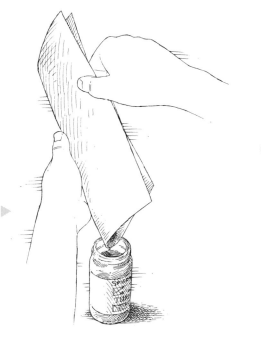

Spices
APPLYING SEASONINGS TO A ROAST

To ensure that meat is well seasoned, it's important to apply seasonings evenly. This is especially important when coating a roast with cracked peppercorns or a spice rub for grilling. Here's how we apply seasonings to beef tenderloin, pork loin, and other large roasts before cooking.

Set the roast on a sheet of plastic wrap and rub it all over with a little oil. Sprinkle with salt, pepper, or other spices, then lift the plastic wrap up and around the meat to press on the excess.

Spices
REMOVING SPICES EASILY

Some soup or sauce recipes call for cooking spices and herbs in the liquid and then removing them before serving. Instead of fishing around for black peppercorns, cloves, star anise, bay leaves, or garlic, try this tip.

Place the spices in a mesh tea ball and then drop the closed ball into the pot. Hang the chain over the side of the pot for easy removal.

Splatter Screen
IMPROVISING WITH WIRE-MESH STRAINER

Splatter screens are handy when frying, but if your kitchen doesn't have one, try this substitute.

An overturned wire-mesh strainer of the appropriate diameter will work just as well.

Squash
CUTTING WITH A CLEAVER AND MALLET

Tip 489

Winter squash are notoriously difficult to cut. Even the best chef's knives can struggle with their thick skins and odd shapes. We prefer to use a cleaver and mallet when working with large winter squash.

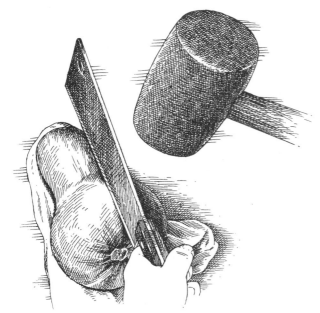

❶ Set the squash on a damp kitchen towel to hold it in place. Position the cleaver on the skin of the squash.

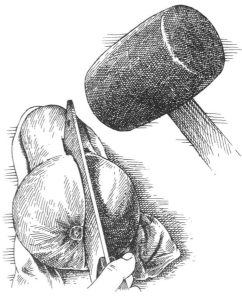

❷ Strike the back of the cleaver with a mallet to drive the cleaver deep into the squash. Continue to hit the cleaver with the mallet until the cleaver cuts through the squash and opens it up.

Squash
REMOVING SEEDS

Tip 490

Digging through the cavity of a winter squash to remove seeds and strings can be tedious, even with a large spoon. Here's a better way to ready squash for cooking.

Use an ice cream scoop with a curved bowl to cut out all the seeds and strings without damaging the flesh. Because the edge on this kind of scoop is very sharp, it cuts easily, and because the scoop is larger than a spoon, it can remove more seeds in a single swipe.

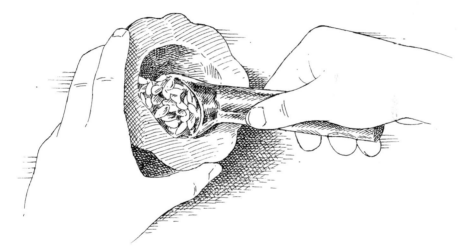

Steaming
PREVENTING SCORCHED PANS

When using just a little bit of water and a steamer basket, it's easy to let the pot run dry, causing a potentially dangerous situation. When steaming foods that take a long time to cook, such as artichokes, here's how to figure out when the pot needs more water.

Before cooking, place a few glass marbles in the bottom of the pan. Add the water and the steamer basket, cover, and cook as usual. When the water level drops too low, the marbles will begin to rattle around, and the racket will remind you to add more water.

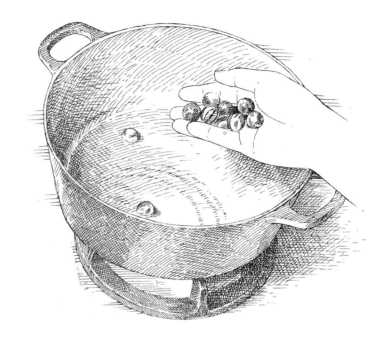

Stews
CUTTING YOUR OWN MEAT

Packages of "stew meat" sold in supermarkets often contain misshapen scraps of varying sizes. For even cooking, pieces should be 1½-inch cubes.

Buy a boneless roast (from the chuck for beef stew) and cut it into chunks yourself. This way you can also trim excess bits of fat and gristle.

Stews
DEFATTING WITH A LETTUCE LEAF

It's easy enough to remove excess fat from a brothy soup in a flash—use a gravy separator. With a chunky stew, this method just won't work.

Instead, place a large lettuce leaf on the surface of the stew; it will absorb excess fat, and you can then remove and discard the leaf.

Stir-Frying
JUDGING THE HEAT LEVEL IN THE PAN

We find that a large nonstick skillet works better than a wok when stir-frying on an American stove. The flat bottom of the skillet fits better with conventional burners, and the pan gets hot all over. A wok is designed to rest in a conical pit where flames can heat all sides. On a stove, only the bottom of a wok really gets hot. This is a problem because stir-frying demands a lot of heat.

When the ingredients are ready, set the skillet over high heat for several minutes. To see if the pan is hot enough, hold your hand an inch above the pan. When the pan is so hot you can keep your hand there for only 3 seconds, add the oil, heat it briefly, and then start cooking.

One of the biggest complaints home cooks have about stir-fries is that the garlic and ginger can burn and give the food a burnt, harsh flavor. Instead of adding the garlic and ginger at the start of the cooking process, try this method.

Stir-Frying
ADDING GARLIC AND GINGER

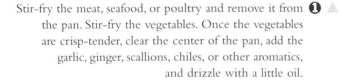

Stir-fry the meat, seafood, or poultry and remove it from ❶ ▲ the pan. Stir-fry the vegetables. Once the vegetables are crisp-tender, clear the center of the pan, add the garlic, ginger, scallions, chiles, or other aromatics, and drizzle with a little oil.

Use a wok shovel/spatula to ❷ ▶ mash the garlic and ginger as they cook. After about 10 seconds, stir the garlic and ginger mixture into the vegetables, add the seared meat, seafood, or poultry along with the sauce, and finish cooking.

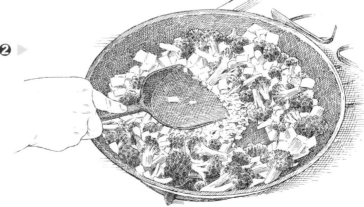

Strawberries
HULLING

Early-season strawberries can have tough, white cores that are best removed. If you don't own a strawberry huller, you can improvise with a plastic drinking straw.

Push the straw through the bottom of the berry and up through the leafy stem end. The straw will remove the core as well as the leafy top.

When cooking a stuffed chicken or turkey, it's important to measure the temperature of the stuffing as well as the bird. Stuffing is fully cooked and safe to eat at 165 degrees.

Insert an instant-read thermometer into the center of the cavity to measure the internal temperature of the stuffing.

Stuffing
TAKING THE TEMPERATURE

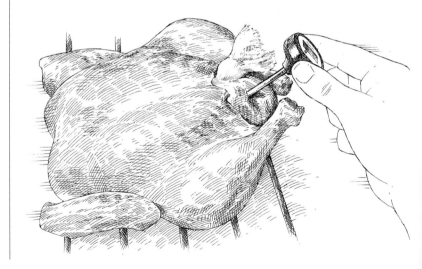

Tartlets – Zucchini

Tartlets
FILLING INDIVIDUAL SHELLS

Filling individual shells with a custard or other filling can be both messy and tedious. To fill the shells with speed and precision, use a bulb baster.

❶ Place the filling in a measuring cup, then fill the bulb baster from the cup.

Move the bulb baster directly ❷ over the tartlet shell and squirt out just the right amount of filling. Repeat until all the shells are filled.

Sweet tart pastry, called pâte sucrée, can be sticky—as can regular pie dough. Instead of coating the work surface with a thick layer of flour (which will just make the dough dry and crumbly), use this method for rolling out sticky dough.

Tarts
ROLLING THE DOUGH

Place the chilled dough ❶ ▲ round between two sheets of plastic wrap. Roll the dough outward from the center with even pressure.

When the dough has reached ❷ ▶ the desired size, peel off the top sheet of plastic, flip the dough into the tart pan, then peel off the second sheet of plastic.

The edges of a tart shell
should be flush with
the rim on the pan.
Here's how to remove
excess dough.

Once the dough has
been fitted into the tart pan,
run a rolling pin over the
top of the pan to break
off any dough that rises
above the rim.

Tarts
LEVELING THE EDGES

Tart dough that has
been rolled out and fitted
into a tart pan can be
refrigerated for a day or
two or frozen for several
months. Here's how we
protect the delicate
pastry from picking up
off flavors or falling
victim to freezer burn.

An 8- or 9-inch unbaked
tart shell can be slipped right
into a gallon-sized zipper-
lock plastic bag. Seal the
bag and then refrigerate
or freeze as desired.

Tarts
STORING AN UNBAKED SHELL

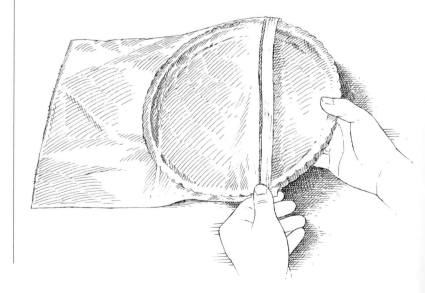

Tip 502

Tarts
PROTECTING THE EDGES FROM BURNING

Sometimes the edges of a tart shell can burn before the bottom is cooked through and nicely browned. Instead of covering the edges of the tart shell with aluminum foil, here's a simple way to protect the crust.

If you notice that the edges are browning too quickly, invert the ring from a second, larger tart pan, place it over the endangered crust, and continue baking.

Tarts
EASY UNMOLDING

Once a tart has baked and cooled, you need to remove the outer ring. Lifting up the removable pan bottom with your hand, causes the ring to slide down your arm like a Hula Hoop. Here's an easy way to remove the ring, without any complicated maneuvers.

Set a wide, stout can, such as a 28-ounce tomato can, on a flat surface. Set the cooled tart and pan on top of the can. Hold the pan ring and gently pull it downward—the can will support the pan base and the tart as you remove the ring.

Tarts
IMPROVISED COVER

A footed cake stand is probably the best plate for serving a baked tart. But what about the leftovers? A cake stand won't fit in most refrigerators.

Place the tart, still on the removable pan bottom, in the refrigerator. Invert a springform pan and place it over the tart. The tart will be protected and you can stack items on top of the springform pan.

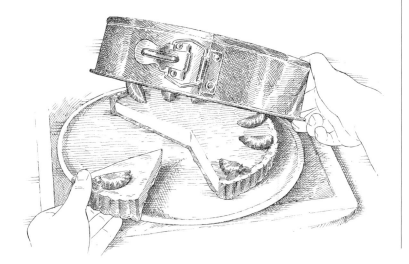

Tip 505

A pitcher of iced tea requires the use of several tea bags. To keep the tea from tasting bitter, the bags should be removed after steeping for 3 minutes. Here's an easy way to remove the tea bags without having to reach into the hot liquid.

Tea
REMOVING TEA BAGS

Tie the tea bag strings **❶** ▷ together, then slide a bamboo skewer or single chopstick through the knot before tightening it.

Position the skewer across the **❷** ▷ top of the pan with the tea bags immersed in the water. When the tea is finished brewing, lift the skewer up and away, and you'll take the spent tea bags with it.

Tomatoes
CORING

Tip 506

Tomatoes are almost always cored—that is, the tough stem is removed and discarded. Before chopping or slicing a tomato, we always core it. We also suggest coring before peeling because coring provides a practical point of departure when it's time to peel.

Place the tomato on its side on a work surface. Holding the tomato stable with one hand, insert the tip of a paring knife about 1 inch into the tomato at an angle just outside the core. Move the paring knife with a sawing motion, at the same time rotating the tomato toward you until the core is cut free.

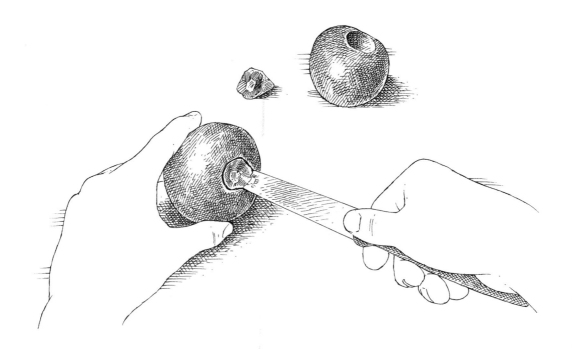

Unless you have a very
sharp knife, tomato skin
can resist the knife edge
and the tomato becomes
crushed. Here's a trick
that starts with a cored
tomato.

Tomatoes
SLICING

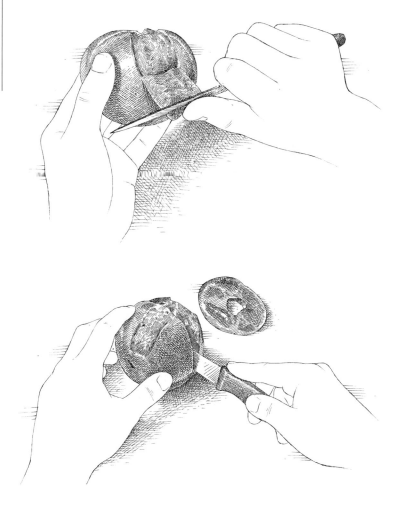

❶ Use a paring knife to
remove a strip of skin from
the exposed core area down
to the blossom end of
the tomato.

❷ Slice the tomato along the
skinned strip so that the knife
does not have to cut through
skin before it can enter
the tomato.

Tomatoes
PEELING

There are many recipes that call for peeling fresh tomatoes. If left on, the peels can separate from the flesh and roll up into hard, unappetizing bits when the tomatoes are cooked. Here's how to get rid of the skins on standard round tomatoes as well as on oblong plum, or Roma, tomatoes.

❶ Place cored tomatoes in boiling water, no more than 5 at a time. Boil until skins split and begin to curl around the cored area of the tomato, about 15 seconds for very ripe tomatoes or up to 30 seconds for firmer, underripe ones. Remove the tomatoes from the water with a slotted spoon or mesh skimmer and place them in a bowl of ice water to stop the cooking process and cool the tomatoes.

❷ With a paring knife, peel the skins using the curled edges at the core as your point of departure. (The bowl of ice water serves a helpful second function—the skins will slide right off the blade of the knife if you dip the blade into the water.)

Tomatoes
SEEDING

The seeds are watery and sometimes bitter and are often removed before chopping a tomato. These techniques work for both peeled and unpeeled tomatoes. Note that because of their different shapes, round and plum (also called Roma) tomatoes are seeded differently.

Tip 509

To seed a round tomato, halve the cored tomato along the equator. If the tomato is ripe and juicy, gently give it a squeeze and shake out the seeds and gelatinous material. If not, scoop them out with your finger or a small spoon.

Tip 510

To seed an oblong plum tomato, halve the cored tomato lengthwise, cutting through the core end. Cut through the inner membrane with a paring knife or break through it with your finger and scoop out the seeds and gelatinous material.

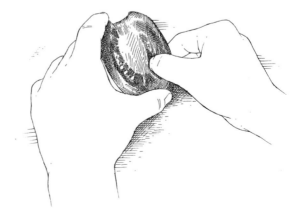

Tomatoes

NEATLY CHOPPING CANNED TOMATOES

Tip 511

Chopping juicy canned tomatoes can be a messy job, but it needn't be if you use this trick.

Pour the canned tomatoes into a bowl and use a pastry blender to "chop" them.

Tip 512

Tongs

STORING SAFELY

We love spring-loaded tongs for turning foods in skillets and on the grill. But put those tongs in a small drawer with other tools, and they can cause chaos. The tongs can become tangled with other tools and can even prevent the drawer from opening. Here's a safe way to store spring-loaded tongs.

Slide the closed tongs into the cardboard tube from a roll of plastic wrap. The tongs can then be stored in the drawer without opening or interfering with other tools.

Tongs

CADDY FOR COOKING

Tip 513

The splay of tongs makes them unsuitable for placing on a spoonrest while cooking. We like this space-saving alternative to catching drips and spills.

Place the tongs in a heavy beer or coffee mug to keep your stovetop or counter clean.

Tip 514

The tortillas sold in bulk packages at warehouse-type supermarkets are much less expensive than the smaller packages sold at the grocery store. But if you freeze the whole package, you'll end up ripping many tortillas as you try to free just a couple from the frozen block.

Tortillas

BULK STORAGE

Before freezing, separate the tortillas with sheets of wax or parchment paper. Place the stack of separated tortillas in freezer bags and freeze as usual. The paper dividers make it easy to pull individual tortillas from the frozen pile.

Turkey
BRINING OUT OF THE REFRIGERATOR

Tip 515

For years, we've advocated soaking a turkey in a saltwater bath before roasting. This process, called brining, produces a moist, well-seasoned bird. The problem is where to keep the turkey as it brines. A stockpot or clean bucket large enough to hold a turkey, 2 gallons of cold water, and salt simply won't fit in most refrigerators. A cold basement or garage can be used. When those options are not available, try this method.

Line a large stockpot or clean bucket with a turkey-sized oven bag. Place several large, clean, frozen ice-gel packs in the brine with the turkey. Tie the bag shut, cover the container, and place in a cool spot for 4 hours. Because of the short brining time, you must use a lot of salt—either 2 cups of table salt or 4 cups of kosher salt. Once the turkey is brined, remember to rinse the bird well under running water and pat dry with paper towels.

Turkey
REMOVING PART OF THE WINGS

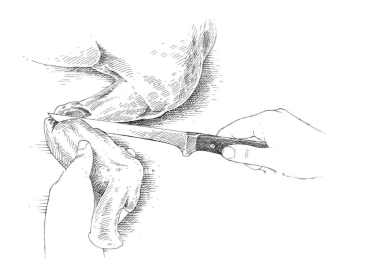

Large turkeys can hang over the sides of even the largest roasting pan and drip fat onto the oven floor. Here's how to keep your kitchen smoke-free and get some extra parts to make gravy.

Remove the first two joints of the wing, leaving only the drumette attached to the bird. Reserve the wings for use along with the neck, tail, and giblets when making gravy.

Once the bird has been stuffed, you must close the cavity to prevent the stuffing from spilling out.

Cut wooden skewers into four pieces, each about 5 inches long. Push the skewers through the skin on either side of the cavity. Use a 20-inch piece of heavy kitchen twine to lace the cavity shut, as if lacing a pair of boots.

Turkey
TRUSSING THE CAVITY SHUT

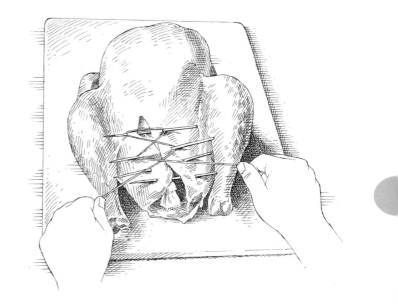

Turkey
KNOWING WHEN IT'S DONE

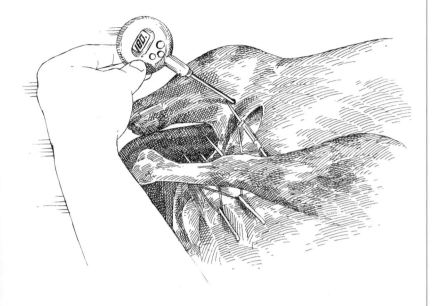

For many cooks, the hardest part of preparing Thanksgiving dinner is figuring out when to take the turkey out of the oven. Use an instant-read thermometer properly, and you will never overcook a turkey again.

The breast is ready when cooked to an internal temperature of 160 degrees. However, the thighs are not really done until they reach an internal temperature of 175 to 180 degrees. For this reason, take the internal temperature of the bird in the thickest part of the thigh, as shown.

Turkey
EASY TURNING

Many recipes for roasting turkey call for turning the turkey halfway through cooking. Care must be taken when lifting and turning a hot turkey.

Slip clean plastic produce bags over large oven mitts. The plastic will keep the mitts from getting greasy and there's no chance of your burning your hands.

Turkey
LEVERAGED LIFTING

Transferring a hot turkey from the roasting rack onto the carving board can be a messy, precarious maneuver. We find that two long-handled wooden spoons make this job easier.

Insert the bowl ends of the spoons into either end of the bird's cavity so that the handles stick out. Grasp the handles, really choking up on them so your hands are right next to the turkey, and lift the bird off the rack.

When tying meat, you
want to keep the ball of
butcher's twine away from
the raw food.

Place the twine on the
handle of a meat pounder to
prevent contamination of
the entire spool.

Twine
KEEPING IT CLEAN

Twine
PRACTICING BUTCHER'S KNOTS

Many cooks have
trouble tying roasts
properly. Here's a clean
way to practice your
knotting skills.

Tie strands of butcher's twine
around a roll of paper towels.
Once your have mastered the
art of knotting, it's time to
move on to food.

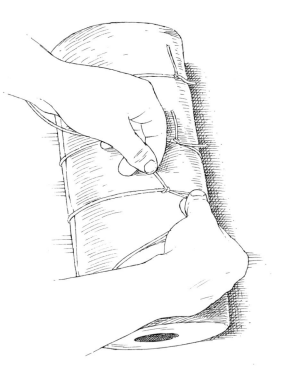

V-Rack
SECURING TO ROASTING PAN

Tip 523

If your V-rack and your roasting pan are not well matched in size, or if you have a nonstick roasting pan, the V-rack and its heavy contents can slide around the pan and create a dangerous situation. Here's how to stabilize a slippery rack.

Make four ropes of twisted aluminum foil and twist two onto each end of the V-rack base. Feed the free ends of the ropes through the pan handles and twist to fasten them around the handles.

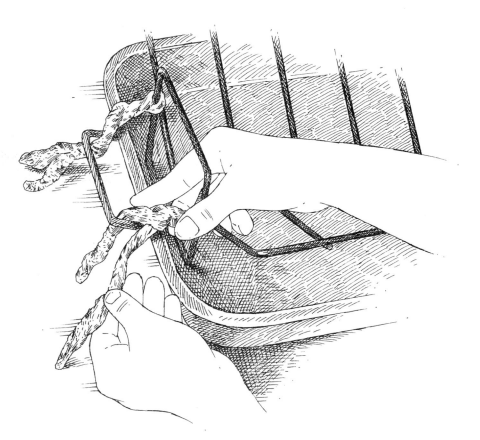

V-Rack

STABILIZING ON THE GRILL

Tip 524

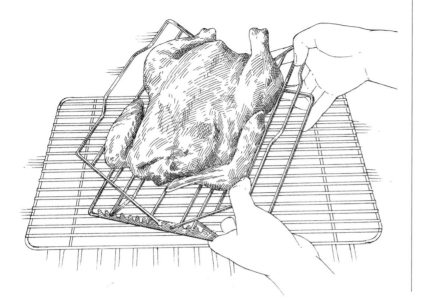

A turkey roasted on the grill can be delicious. But the skin can burn if the turkey is cooked right on the grate. We prefer to elevate the bird in a V-rack. However, the base of some V-racks may slip through the bars on your grill grate.

Cover the grill grate with a wire cooling rack for baking so that its bars run perpendicular to the bars on the grill grate. The cooling rack provides a stable surface on which the base of the V-rack can rest.

Tip 525

A vanilla bean adds the truest flavor to ice cream, custards, and puddings. The seeds inside the bean have the most flavor. Here's how to free the seeds from the pod.

Vanilla

REMOVING SEEDS FROM A BEAN

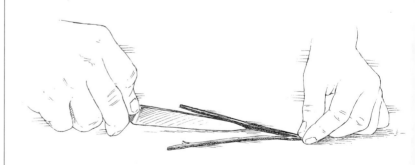

▲ ❶ Use a small, sharp knife to cut the vanilla bean in half lengthwise.

Steamed vegetables can
cool off quickly. Here's a
way to slow the process.

Vegetables
WARMING THE SERVING BOWL

When steaming vegetables,
invert a heat-proof serving
bowl over the steaming pot
so it will heat up while
the vegetables cook.

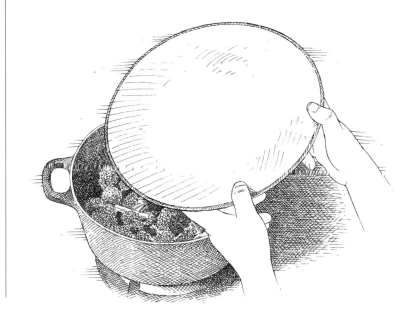

❷ Place the knife at one end of one bean half and press down to
flatten the bean as you move the knife away from you and catch
the seeds on the edge of the blade. Add the seeds as well as the
pods to the liquid ingredients.

A paring knife can be
used to restore the edge
on a dulled peeler.

Vegetable Peeler
SHARPENING

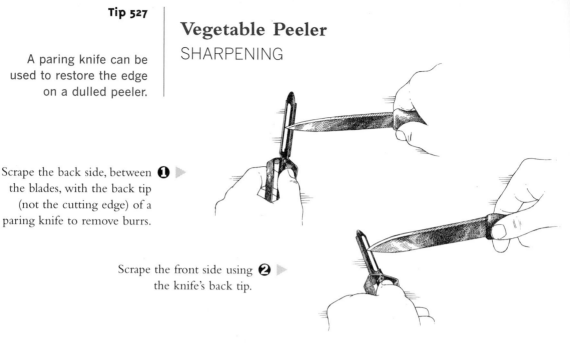

Scrape the back side, between ❶ ▷
the blades, with the back tip
(not the cutting edge) of a
paring knife to remove burrs.

Scrape the front side using ❷ ▷
the knife's back tip.

Waffle Iron
CLEANING

The nonstick surface of
most waffle irons is easy
to clean, but getting in
between the ridges of the
iron can be a challenge.

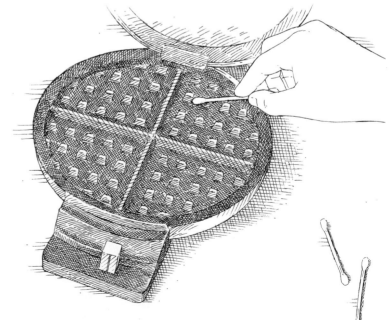

Cotton swabs are just the
right size to wipe away
residue in between the
iron's ridges.

Walnuts
SKINNING

The skins from toasted walnuts can impart a bitter taste to dishes. Here's a simple way to remove these thin skins.

Once the nuts have been toasted, rub them inside a clean kitchen towel. The skins will separate from the nut meats.

Water Bath
MAKESHIFT BASE

Many recipes for baking individual custards recommend lining the water bath pan with a kitchen towel to insulate and cushion the ramekins, but this leaves you with a sopping wet towel.

Instead, line the water bath pan with a nonstick baking mat (called a Silpat). The mat will keep the ramekins in place and, unlike a towel, won't need to be wrung out or laundered.

Wine Bottle
FISHING OUT CORK CRUMBS

Few things are more frustrating than fishing out bits of cork that have fallen into a freshly opened bottle of wine. If you're tired of this task, try this ingenious trick.

Insert a plastic drinking straw into the neck of the opened bottle and over the cork crumb, then place a finger over the end of the straw and lift it out. A vacuum is created in the straw that traps the cork crumb along with a little wine.

Wine Glasses
DRYING ON CHOPSTICKS

With one wrong move or an inadvertent bump, a dish rack filled with drying dishes can wreak havoc on delicate stemware. Here's a good way to dry glasses in a safe corner of the counter, out of harm's way.

Set up chopsticks (the square-sided kind are best) parallel to each other and about 1½ to 2 inches apart on the counter. Place the wet glasses on the chopsticks to dry. The slight elevation off the counter allows air to circulate into the glasses and speeds drying.

Zucchini
GRATING

Many recipes call for salting zucchini before cooking to rid it of excess water. Drier zucchini browns better and tastes better. However, there's not always time to salt zucchini and wait for an hour or two. Here's a quick way to remove excess water. You can also use this technique for yellow summer squash.

❶ Shred the zucchini on the large holes of a box grater or in a food processor fitted with the shredding disk.

❷ Wrap the shredded zucchini in paper towels and squeeze out as much liquid as possible. When dry, the zucchini is ready to be cooked.

Tip 534

When making stuffed
zucchini, it is necessary
to scoop out the seeds
with a spoon. In fresh
zucchini, the seeds and
flesh can be very firm,
making this job difficult.
Here's an easy way to
loosen up the seeds.
This tip also works
with eggplant.

Zucchini
SEEDING

▲ **1** Place the zucchini on a work
surface and roll, applying slight
pressure with your hands. The
pressure will soften the insides
and loosen the seeds.

▼ **2** Halve the rolled zucchini
lengthwise and scoop out the
seeds with a spoon.

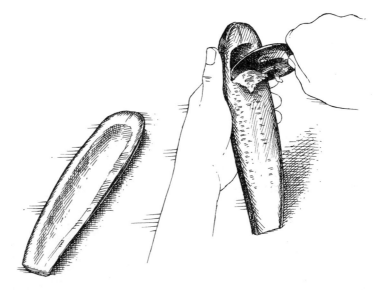

INDEX

A

ACIDULATED WATER
freezing spent lemon shells for, 245

ALMOND PASTE
softening, 2

ALMONDS
decorating cakes with, 69

ALUMINUM FOIL:
cleaning grill grates with, 188
flame tamers improvised with, 156–57
protecting edges of pie crusts with, 306
storing boxes of, 216
wood chip packets made with, 187

ANCHOVIES
mincing, 3

APPLES:
baking, 4
coring, 4, 5

APPLIANCES:
blenders, cleaning, 31
coffee grinders, grinding evenly with, 103
coffee machines, melting chocolate in, 100
garbage disposals, improvised traps for, 168
hair dryers:
creating silky look on frosting with, 67
restarting grill fires with, 183
heavy, moving, 261
immersion blenders:
shortcutting frozen juice preparation with, 273
smoothing out lumps in polenta with, 314
microwave ovens:
cleaning, 258
storing flour in, 158
waffle irons, cleaning, 384

APPLIANCES *(cont.)*
washing machines, keeping beverages chilled in, 26
See also Dishwashers; Food processors; Mixers

ARTICHOKES
steaming, 6

ASH
removing from grill, 193

ASPARAGUS
trimming tough ends of, 7

AVOCADOS:
mashing for guacamole, 194
peeling and slicing, 9
pitting, 8
testing for ripeness, 7

B

BACON:
drippings
removing from pan, 11
saving for another use, 10–11
storing, 10

BAGELS
shaping stiff dough into rings, 12

BAKEWARE:
bread pans, improvised, 35
greasing and flouring, 14
Silpat (nonstick baking mats), lining water baths with, 385
springform pans, tart covers improvised with, 368
tart pan bottoms, flipping hash browns with, 196
utensils, drying quickly, 220
See also Baking sheets; Cooling racks; Loaf pans; Muffin tins; Parchment paper; Ramekins; Tube pans

BAKING POWDER
testing for freshness, 15

BAKING SHEETS:
arranging cookie dough on, 107
as extra-large trivets, 224

BAKING SHEETS *(cont.)*
keeping stovetop clean with, 224
for multiple batches of cookies, 110
rotating, 109
slip-free parchment paper for, 14
storing, 216

BAKING TIPS:
keeping track of dry ingredients, 13
measuring liquids, 13
mess-free baker's coating, 14
slip-free parchment paper, 14

BALSAMIC VINEGAR
tinting hard-cooked eggs with, 146

BAMBOO SKEWERS:
soaking, 191
See also Skewers

BANANAS
overripe, saving for bread, 16

BARBECUE SAUCE
applying with squeeze bottle, 16

BASIL:
alternate uses for, 202
releasing oils from, 17
storing, 201

BASTING BRUSHES:
cleaning, 48
improvised, 190–91

BEAN SPROUTS
storing, 17

BEATERS
lemon reamers improvised with, 241

BEEF:
burgers, checking temperature of, 48–49
kebabs, preparing meat for, 18
prime rib, tying, 18
steak(s):
checking temperature of, 19
Philly, sandwiches, preparing meat for, 22

BEEF *(cont.)*
  steak(s)
    slicing for stir-fries, 23
    T-bone, grilling evenly, 20
    T-bone, slicing, 21
  tenderloin:
    removing silver skin from, 24
    tying, 24–25
  See also Meat

BEETS
  removing stains from, 25

BERRIES
  mixing gently, 26

BEVERAGES:
  cappuccino, foaming milk for, 76
  freezing lemon slices for, 240
  Gibsons, chilling, 102
  iced tea, removing tea bags
    from, 369
  keeping chilled, 26
  lemonade, mashing sliced
    lemons for, 244
  orange juice, preparing from
    frozen concentrate, 273

BISCOTTI
  quick drying on rack, 27

BISCUITS:
  coating cutters for, 161
  splitting for shortcakes, 29
  wedge method for, 28

BLANCHING:
  greens, removing excess
    water after, 179
  shocking vegetables after, 29

BLENDERS:
  cleaning face of, 31
  cleaning jar of, 30
  See also Immersion blenders

BOK CHOY
  slicing whites and greens of, 32

BOTTLE CAPS
  hard-to-open, 231

BOTTLE OPENERS
  opening tightly sealed jars
    with, 228

BOUQUET GARNI, 199

BOWLS:
  chilling, for whipping cream, 131
  keeping in place during mixing,
    259
  metal, keeping roast warm
    under, 254
  sauce, stabilizing, 204
  serving. *See* Serving dishes

BREAD:
  crumbs, homemade, 42
  foccacia, dimpling dough for, 161
  keeping fresh, 33
  making. *See* Bread-making tips
  quick, making sling for, 41
  saving overripe bananas for, 16
  slicing crusty loaves of, 33
  softening almond paste with, 2
  softening brown sugar with, 45
  spreading butter on corn
    with, 125
  stale, freshening, 34

BREADING CHICKEN CUTLETS:
  mess-free, 92
  stabilizing coating, 93

BREAD-MAKING TIPS:
  adding flour to dough:
    with food processor, 160
    judging when enough, 36
  checking temperature in
    loaf pan, 40
  improvising pans, 35
  measuring dough, 38
  rising:
    covering dough during, 36
    draft-free, in loaf pan, 37
    tracking volume change in, 39
  slashing proofed loaf, 40

BRINING POULTRY:
  out of refrigerator, 376
  rinsing after, 324

BROCCOLI
  cutting into florets, 42–43

BROTH
  canned, defatting, 44

BROWNIES
  easy removal of, 47

BROWN SUGAR:
  softening, 45
  storing and measuring, 46

BRUSHES:
  basting, improvised, 190–91
  cleaning, 48
  nail, cleaning blenders with, 31
  scrubbing clams with, 101

BULB BASTERS
  filling tartlet shells with, 364

BURGERS
  checking temperature of, 48–49

BUTCHER'S KNOTS
  practicing, 380

BUTTER DISHES
  storing goat cheese in, 81

BUTTERFLYING CHICKEN, 87

BUTTER(S):
  compound, shaping and
    freezing, 50
  grating into flour, 52
  shaving thin slices of, over
    casseroles, 51
  softened:
    in a hurry, 54
    measured tablespoons of, 49
    visual cues for, 53
  spreading on corn, 125

C

CABBAGE:
  cutting through big head of, 56
  shredding, 57–58

CAKE PANS
  greasing and flouring, 14

CAKES:
  batter for:
    dividing, 59
    filling tube pans with, 59
  coffee, drizzling with white
    icing, 104
  cover for, improvised, 74
  decorating:
    with chocolate shavings, 70
    dusting flourless chocolate
      cake, 73
    with nuts, 69
    removing stencils after, 72
    with two-tone pattern, 68
    writing on frosting, 71
  deep, testing for doneness, 62
  frosting:
    aligning layers and, 63
    anchoring bottom layer
      and, 64
    creating silky look in, 67
    getting top layer in place
      and, 65
    putting pattern in icing, 66
  lining pan and serving plate
    for, 60–61
  rotating during baking, 60
  transporting, 75

CAN OPENERS
  cleaning, 76

CAPPUCCINO
  foaming milk for, 76

CARROTS
cutting into julienne, 77

CARVING
steadying roast for, 255

CASSEROLES:
checking temperature of, 232
shaving thin slices of butter over, 51

CAULIFLOWER
cutting into florets, 78

CELERY
chopping quickly, 79

CELERY ROOT
removing thick peel of, 79

CHARCOAL:
building two-level fire with, 186
lighting, 181, 184–85
measuring, 183
preparing in advance, 182

CHEESE:
goat:
slicing, 81
storing, 81
hard, cutting safely, 80
mozzarella, slicing, 83
Parmesan, shaving, 80
semisoft, shredding, 82

CHEESECLOTH
grilling whole fish in, 154

CHERRIES
pitting, 84

CHICKEN:
bone-in breasts, grilling, 98
brined, rinsing, 324
butterflied, grilling, 88
butterflying, 87
checking temperature of, 89
checking temperature of stuffing in, 362
cutlets:
breading without mess, 92
cutting into uniform pieces, 95
keeping breading firmly attached to, 93
pounding, 91
sautéing safely, 94
trimming fat and tendons from, 90
kebabs, skewering meat for, 96
legs, separating thighs and drumsticks of, 96

CHICKEN *(cont.)*
raw:
getting grip on, 84
seasoning safely, 86
washing and drying, 85
seasoning:
with lemon, 86
safety concerns and, 86
vertical roasters for, improvised, 88
wings, preparing for cooking, 97

CHILES
chipotle, in adobo sauce, freezing, 99

CHILLING:
beverages in washing machine, 26
bowls for whipping cream, 131
Gibsons, 102
soups quickly, 346

CHIMNEY STARTERS:
lighting fire with, 181
lighting fire without, 184
making your own, 184–85

**CHIPOTLE CHILES
IN ADOBO SAUCE**
freezing, 99

CHOCOLATE:
cake, flourless, dusting, 73
cocoa powder, decorating cakes with, 68
melting in drip coffee machine, 100
shavings, decorating cakes with, 70
writing on frosted cakes with, 71

CHOPPING:
canned tomatoes, 374
celery, 79
fennel seeds, 152
nuts:
neatly, 268
quickly, 267

CHOPSTICKS
drying wine glasses on, 386

CILANTRO
storing, 201

CINNAMON ROLLS
cutting, 100

CLAMS:
scrubbing with brush, 101
straining precious liquid from, 101

CLEANING:
beet stains, 25
blenders, 30–31
brushes, 48
can openers, 76
copper, 123
food processor workbowls, 164
garlic presses, 172
grill grates without brush, 188
microwave ovens, 258
pots and pans, 122
spilled oil, 225
waffle irons, 384

CLEAVERS
cutting winter squash with mallets and, 356

COCKTAILS:
Gibsons, chilling, 102
improvised shakers for, 102

COCOA POWDER
decorating cakes with, 68

COFFEE
foaming milk for (cappuccino), 76

COFFEE CAKES
drizzling with white icing, 104

COFFEE FILTERS:
making bouquet garni with, 199
as mise en place cups, 218
stabilizing, 103

COFFEE GRINDERS
grinding evenly with, 103

COFFEE MACHINES
melting chocolate in, 100

COFFEE MUGS:
with lids, cocktail shakers improvised with, 102
mortars and pestles improvised with, 262

COLANDERS:
improvised with steamer basket, 105
keeping pancakes warm under, 278
washing raw chicken in, 85

COLORED SUGAR
making your own, 115

COOKIE JARS
keeping cookies fresh in, 118

POTS
See Cookware

POT SCRUBBERS
securing small items in
dishwasher with, 136

POULTRY:
brined, rinsing, 324
Cornish hens, preventing
ballooning of, 129
duck:
preparing for grilling, 138
rendering fat from, 177
goose, rendering fat from, 177
See also Chicken; Turkey

PRETZEL STICKS
as edible toothpicks for
hors d'oeuvres, 203

PROPANE TANKS
checking fuel level in, 180

R

RAMEKINS:
keeping stuffed peppers
upright in, 297
lining water baths for, 385
removing from water baths, 134

RAVIOLI
impromptu wrappers for, 326

RECIPES
protecting in kitchen, 327

**REDUCING SAUCES AND STOCKS
ACCURATELY,** 338

REMOTE CONTROLS
keeping clean, 223

RHUBARB
peeling, 330

RICE:
keeping salt shakable with, 336
rinsing, 328
steaming for fluffy texture, 329

RISING DOUGH:
covering during, 36
draft-free, in loaf pan, 37
tracking volume change in, 39

ROLLING PINS:
crushing peppercorns with, 290
improvised, 300
moving pie dough on, 301
releasing flavorful oils
from basil with, 17

ROSEMARY
adding flavor of, 198

RUBBER BANDS:
around tong tips for
sure grip, 134
opening tightly sealed
jars with, 228
tracking dough rise with, 39

S

SAFFRON
crumbling to release flavor, 331

SAGE
storing, 201

SALADS:
draining pasta for, 282
Jell-O, unmolding, 212

SALAD SPINNERS:
cake covers improvised with, 74
drying tomato slices in, 311
getting better leverage with, 331
spinning greens drier with, 332

SALMON:
fillets:
removing pinbones from, 333
turning into steaks, 334
side of, removing pinbones
from, 332

SALT:
cleaning brushes with, 48
extracting moisture from
cucumbers with, 133
mincing garlic to paste with, 173
removing beet stains with, 25

SALT BOXES
easy pull-tabs for, 335

SALT SHAKERS:
flouring with, 159
keeping salt shakable in, 336

SANDWICHES:
fresh herbs in, 202
overstuffed, stabilizing, 336
Philly steak, preparing
meat for, 22

SANDWICH PRESSES
improvised, 337

SAUCES:
barbecue, applying with
squeeze bottle, 16
defatting, 339
pesto, releasing flavorful
oils from basil for, 17

SAUCES (cont.)
reducing accurately, 338
removing spices from,
before serving, 355

SAUTÉING:
chicken cutlets, 94
double duty for pot lids in, 226
minimizing splatter from,
224, 226

SCALLIONS
slicing with scissors, 340

SCALLOPS:
grilling, 341
removing tendons from, 340

SCISSORS:
for clipping herbs in garden, 200
cutting pizza with, 313
slicing scallions with, 340

SERVING DISHES:
for cake, keeping neat, 60–61
for grilled foods, double
duty for, 192
keeping spotless between
uses, 221
for mashed potatoes,
warming, 320
for vegetables, warming, 383

SHALLOTS
mincing, 341

SHARPENING:
knives, determining honing
angle for, 235
vegetable peelers, 384

SHELLFISH:
clams:
scrubbing with brush, 101
straining precious liquid
from, 101
lobsters:
controlling mess from, 250
hard-shells versus soft-shells, 249
mussels, debearding, 267
oysters, shucking, 276
scallops:
grilling, 341
removing tendons from, 340
shrimp:
deveining with shells on, 343
grilling, 344
soft-shell crabs, cleaning, 130

SHELVES
homemade tiered, 214

SHOCKING VEGETABLES, 29